This autographed book
by

Dr. Toyozo W. Nakarai

Emmanuel's Honored Professor
of
Old Testament

is presented to

First Christian Church

In appreciation for interest
and
support during the year 1971

leuyozo W. nakarai

emmanuel school of religion

AN ELDER'S
PUBLIC PRAYERS

AN ELDER'S
PUBLIC PRAYERS

by

TOYOZO W. NAKARAI

A
Hearthstone
Book

Carlton Press, Inc.   New York, N. Y.

Library of Congress Catalog Card Number: 68-57501

CONTENTS

PREFACE

I have been an elder of a Christian Church, an ordained minister, and a professor of the Bible. Of these three appointments I regard the eldership as the most important, for this responsibility covers every sphere of my life including the ministry and professorship.

As an elder I pray in private and in public. My private prayers are spontaneous, informal and constant. I pray while driving. I pray while lying in bed. I pray while giving counsel. My words are unrefined. My thoughts are not always orderly. I just speak to God, praising Him, thanking Him, confessing to Him, and asking Him to use me, even me, for His cause. Sometimes I ask for His blessings on the people who are in need. Other times I beg Him for health and comfort for the sick and the destitute. In all this, I firmly believe that God responds according to His will, if my prayers are right. The short prayer below is a sample of my private prayers. These are the words that I spoke, when the news of the Japanese attack on Pearl Harbor reached me on December 7, 1941. This prayer has been in my mind ever since. I was born in Japan.

Were I to live tomorrow, I would die for the Christ.
Were I to die tomorrow, I would live for the Christ.

When I am asked to pray in public, and if I am informed of it in time, I put in much time for preparation. I must confess that sometimes this is a cause of agony lasting an entire afternoon and evening, not because the assignment is painful, but because I cannot find the words suitable for the occasion. Other times the thoughts of the expected audience seem to flow into my mind without any effort. In any case, the words that I gather together may be those found in the Bible or other books of a devotional nature, or they may be just those that I use daily. However, for public prayers my expressions are more or less formal. When I complete my first draft, I let my wife look at it, or I read it to her. Then the prayer may be revised according to her reaction. By this time, I have transferred the prayer from paper to my mind; and thus I never read it in public.

The contents of this book are such public prayers that I have used, though I should state that they were not always uttered word for word, for, moved by the Spirit, my expressions may have changed here and there. Just before I pray in public, I always ask God to let me say what He would have me say, and this gives me peace and comfort. At any rate, I acknowledge here the debt I owe to my wife, Frances A. Nakarai, who has been my severe but constructive critic in writing these prayers.

Toyozo W. Nakarai

August 7, 1964
Indianapolis, Indiana

AN ELDER'S
PUBLIC PRAYERS

CHURCH

Church

O Thou, breath of life. Despite the roar of bombing planes and the boom of battering cannons, the rose of Sharon speaketh Thy law and the lily of the valley uttereth Thy love. Lest mankind forget the ultimate creative authorship in Thee, do we humbly dedicate this service to the Christ. Forbid that we pray for miracles and wonders that Thou mayest bestow upon us, but we do ask for steadfast strength and wholehearted consecration equal to our tasks and duties. May the glory of Lebanon displace human distress. May the excellency of Carmel supplant social disorder. May the cross of Jesus dispel worldly disbelief. In our savior's name we pray. Amen.

Note: Written during the war.

* * * *

Our heavenly Father, we thank Thee for Thy grace which has brought us together in order that we may enjoy this fellowship. We thank Thee for the old members of this church, to whom we owe our past experience. We thank Thee for the new members of this church, to whom we owe our future growth. Above all, we thank Thee for the young and the old who are now present, to whom we owe this beautiful demonstration of the unity of ransomed souls. Guide us as we march on towards the perfect image of Christ, and bless our ministers as they wholeheartedly serve Thee and Thy people, to the end that Jesus Christ be glorified. In his name we pray. Amen.

1

Ministry

Our heavenly Father, our trust in Thy promise and our faith in Thy son impel us to place our all in Thy hands. We thank Thee for Thy grace that enables us to serve Thee. We thank Thee for Thy command that enables us to serve Thy creation. Be with us as we abide in Thy name. Yea, let us be with Thee as we preach Thy word. Bless those whom Thou wouldst. May those who suffer for Thy sake feel the embrace of Thy tender love. Amen·

Scripture: Genesis 39:1-6.

Note: "Ministry" means service. A minister is a servant. The word "name" in the Bible sometimes signifies person.

* * * * *

We thank Thee, O Lord, for these holy words that are eternally true. As we stand at the threshold of Thy kingdom, we pray that Thou wilt enable us to be strong and courageous in ferrying Thy people to the promised land. May we not swerve, but may we have confidence in Thee, for Thou art our shield, our refuge, and our redeemer, forever and ever. Amen.

Scripture: Joshua 1:6-9·

Note: Moses, the servant of God, was dead. Joshua, the son of Nun, stood on the eastern bank of the Jordan. There lay before him the promised land. If Palestine were the kingdom of God, we might be compared to Joshua.

Ministry

Our Father in heaven, we thank Thee for the blessed office of Christian ministry. Realizing our inability and many faults, we bow before Thee once again. Grant us intelligence to declare our faith. Give us courage to follow the Christ. Amid the roar of battling cannons, the command of human idols, and the surge of un-Christian forces all over the world, may we each proclaim: "As for me and my people, we will serve the Christ." In his name we pray. Amen.

Scripture: Joshua 24:14-15.

Note: Written during the war. The scripture above contains the words of Joshua's farewell address which he delivered to the Hebrews just before his death. After telling the Hebrews that they should believe in the God of Israel, Joshua left the matter of choice—whether the God of Israel or other gods—to the people; but he said that as for him and his family they would serve the God of Israel.

Ministry

O God, we thank Thee for the light of Thy love that pierces through darkness, for the cross of Thy son that saves all mankind, and for the sheep of Thy fold that Thou hast entrusted unto us. We do not pray for wealth, nor riches, nor honor; but we do pray for Christian wisdom and knowledge. May it be Thy will that Thy sheep be cared for properly. To the shepherd of shepherds, even the Christ, be glory forever and ever. Amen.

Scripture: I Kings 3:5-14.

Note: Upon succeeding his father David, King Solomon made a sacrifice at Gibeon. There, realizing the great responsibility that must be borne by him, the new king prayed for wisdom and knowledge. "Wisdom and knowledge" in this prayer means wisdom and knowledge of God.

Ministry

O God, we now enter into Thy glorious presence, and thank Thee for the New Covenant that Thou hast given us. And lo! We realize that we are "undone," for we are the possessors of "unclean lips" living among the people of "unclean lips." We shrink, but we are ready, O Lord. Cleanse us of our sins by virtue of our faith in Thy Word. We are meek, but we dare, O God· Send us into the most difficult fields, and give us the hardest tasks. Here we are; use us for Thy sake. Amen.

Scripture: Isaiah 6:1-8.

Note: King Menahem of Israel sent a bribe to the Assyrian king in order that his kingship might be safe. King Uzziah of Judah died. Syria and Israel were about to invade Judah; but the material wealth of Judah was blunting the religious consciousness of its people. It was then that the call came to Isaiah.

*   *   *   *   *

We humbly bow before Thee, O Lord, trying to realize the significance of the highest duties and privileges that are ours· We repent with shame, for we have been blind and staggering servants to Thee. Take complete possession of us as we call upon Thee. Break open the sealed Book. May we read therein, not the commandment of man, but the principles of Christian ministry. We ask this in Jesus' name. Amen.

Scripture: Isaiah 29:9-16.

5

Father, we thank Thee for these precious words, more precious than any words of human counsellors. As we meditate upon these thoughts, may our pride vanish, and may we gain that wisdom and that peace. Enable us to dedicate ourselves more fully to the upbuilding of Thy kingdom· Help us to win more souls for Thy sake. In our savior's name we pray. Amen.

Scripture: Proverb 11:2, 11-14, 30-31.

*   *   *   *   *

Oh, Thou, creator of all, who by Thy supreme intelligence brought forth the universe out of chaos, and who by Thy un-excelled wisdom appointed man to rule over Thy creation, we praise Thy name. Help us to become more conscious of Thy divine call and of our sacred mission. Enable us to hear Thy voice. Dispel the darkness within us, and fill us with the light of the cross. May that cross of Jesus endure forever, world without end. Amen.

Scripture: Luke 11:1-14.

Ministry

Mission

Eternal God, for Thy creative wisdom and redemptive grace we praise Thy name. From the earthly dust to the living soul, and from the living soul to the everlasting glory, Thou hast paved the way of the truth. Enable us to find the unlimited riches in whole-hearted sacrifice. Help us to bear the ancient cross in this bewildered world. Grant, O Lord, sufficient power, steadfast virtue, increasing faith, and saintly intelligence to the lives dedicated to Thy missionary cause. Exalted and magnified be Thy golden throne of the Christ. In his name we pray. Amen·

* * * * *

Our Father in heaven, we thank Thee for the Christian conception of the world, its beauty, its goodness, and its trueness. We thank Thee for the Christ, the essence of the harmonious unity of the universe. Enable us to carry on our commission as learners of that teacher, in Goshen, in Nazareth, in Galilee, in Bethlehem, and in any other part of Thy creation. Strengthen our faith as we bear the cross. In Jesus' name we pray. Amen.

Note: "Learners" means disciples.

Ministry

Teaching

Blessed be Thou, O Lord, creator of the universe and Father of mankind. There is none beside Thee. We thank Thee for Thy saving grace enacted by Thy own lamb of Calvary which has brought us to our teaching ministry. As we now assemble here, let us remember the seriousness of the tasks which Thou hast placed in our hands. Let our thoughts be clean. Let our words be pure. Let Thy heavenly wisdom descend upon Thy servants, and let it enlighten our souls. Let it brighten our course. In our savior's name we pray. Amen.

* * * * *

Church and Ministry

Blessed be Thou, O Lord, Father of mankind. With humble hearts and contrite spirits do we invoke Thy blessings upon this assembly. Though mountains fall and oceans surge, let Thy word be our guiding light. Though flowers fade and leaves fall, let the beauty of Thy holiness sanctify our souls. Though nations war and governments rage, let Thy peace be our rock of refuge. Glory be to Thy church. Glory be to Thy ministry. Glory be to the ancient cross. Be with us, O Lord, forever and ever. Amen.

Church and Ministry

O Thou, Master of creation, we thank Thee for the shepherd of shepherds and the lord of lords, even Jesus Christ. We pray for the church universal and for the ministry ecumenical. May Thy church follow the gleam of Thy light. May Thy ministry magnify the glory of the cross. Let Thy church be as strong and firm as the roar of the lion of Judah. Let Thy ministry be as delicate and tender as the fragrance of the lily of the valley. May the smile of goodness prevail over the taunt of evil. May the power of faith overcome the force of death. O great Spirit, we dedicate ourselves to Thee. Let us walk with Thy son through the sweet communion of the saints. In our savior's name. Amen.

Note: "Ecumenical" means universal.

* * * * *

Ordination

O Lord, humbly do we join this laborer of Thy harvest in confessing our faith in the sufficiency of the Christ. Grant him the wealth of Thy spirit and jewel of Thy wisdom. May he bear the torch of Thy gospel and the banner of Thy salvation. Like the prophets of Israel let him speak Thy word. Like the apostles of Thy church let him magnify Thy son. Use him according to Thy will, and guard him against human authorities. Let him feel the surge of the power of Christ now and evermore, to whom be glory, world without end. Amen.

Note: "Gospel" means good news. It may be understood also as God's story.

Installation of Officers

O Lord, we thank Thee for Thy love, so tender and so merciful, that it shields even a bruised reed. We thank Thee for Thy word, so righteous and so true, that it enlightens even this confused world. We thank Thee for these consecrated men and women, so humble and so loyal, that they dedicate even themselves to Thee. May Thy guiding spirit rest upon them, as they serve Thee and Thy children. May now and henceforth these new officers and the rest of us embrace a renewed faith in the Christ, a faith that withstands even the quaking earth and the surging sea. In our savior's name. Amen.

* * * * *

Baptism

For the excellency of Thy handiwork in the heavens above and on earth below, we praise Thy name. We thank Thee for the star over Bethlehem among the luminaries of heaven, and for Thy beloved son among the wonders of earth. May the heavens be opened and the Holy Spirit descend upon those who partake in the initiatory rite of Thy kingdom. And as they march henceforth towards Thy golden throne, may the rod of the shepherd of shepherds protect them, and may his staff sustain them. For we ask through Jesus Christ, our lord. Amen.

Marriage

Blessed be Thou, O God, who from ages past to the ages to come ordained the manner of man and woman to enter the estate of matrimony to multiply themselves, to subdue the earth, and to serve Thee. Be with us as this man and this woman declare before Thee and before these witnesses their cherished faith in each other, dedicating their union to the way of Christ. To him be glory forever and ever. Amen.

* * * * *

Funeral

O Lord, in whose hands rests the destiny of man· Even at a time like this, we praise Thy name. We praise Thy name, for Thou art the healer of the wounded. We praise Thy name, for Thou art the comforter of the bereaved. We thank Thee, for Thou hast released this precious soul from his earthly struggle, transmitted the abundance of the good found in him to his children's children, and hast established thus the living memorial for his sake. But now, O Lord, bless and guide his family and others who knew this beloved soul. Grant them courage, strength, fortitude and peace, with which they may also share the eternal life. Through Jesus Christ, our lord. Amen.

Scriptures: Job 5:18-27; John 14:1-4; I Thessalonians 4:13-18.

11

Funeral

> *Minister*

Praised, exalted, magnified and extolled be Thy name, O God of mercy. Thou hast raised John Smith to be Thy minister. Now Thou hast called him to Thy heavenly realm. We confess our faith victorious which enables us to thank Thee even at a time like this, for his ministry endures forever. As it was to the advantage of his disciples that Jesus passed away, so may it be for the enlightenment of those who knew him that John Smith was taken away. As the snow and storms of the winter foreshadow the flowers and birds of the spring, so may the passing of our beloved minister bespeak the fruitage and harvest of his labors. To this end wilt Thou bless this Thy church, and let our souls declare in the days to come: He lives, he lives, he lives! Through Jesus Christ our lord. Amen.

> *Note: John 16:7 says in part: "... it is for your good that I am going away...."*

* * * * *

Memorial Service

We thank thee, O God, for the Christian faith that pierces through the doubts and fears of human life, and opens for us that vista of eternal life. We thank Thee for the precious lives that have been dedicated at Thy altar for the cause of Christian faith. May our memories of such men help us in the growth of our own Christian wisdom and virtues. Help us to be seekers of the truth, O our redeemer and savior. Amen.

Scripture: Proverb 14:25-34.

Sunday School

Biblical Study

Our Father, we thank Thee for the Book of books that has been handed down unto us by the sages of the past. Watch over us, as we examine ourselves in the light of Thy word. Guide us as we seek for Thy truth. Speak face to face as we yield ourselves unto Thee. Let our thoughts, our words and our acts become acceptable in Thy sight, O our God and our redeemer. Amen.

> *Note: The Bible is a collection of little books. In fact, "Biblia" does mean little books. It is sometimes called the "Book of books" because of its significance. The Jews often identified themselves as "the people of the Book." This has been adopted by Mohammedans and Christians.*

* * * * *

Promotion Day

Mighty God, merciful Father. As another cycle of our educational ministry becomes history, we thank Thee for those who faithfully taught, and for others who earnestly learned. We thank Thee, above all, for the Christ, to whose peace we have been called in one body. Enable us to attune our human peace to his cosmic peace, and let it prevail over us, world without end. Through Jesus Christ, our lord. Amen.

Scripture: Colossians 3:12-17.

Sunday School

Children's Music Program

O God, we thank Thee for our Christian fathers and mothers, our Christian brothers and sisters, and also for all the rest of the members of our Christian families, teachers and friends, for they have brought us up to be Thy children. We thank Thee for the beauty, the liberty, the justice, the wealth, and the abundance of Christian America, for here we may truly practice Christ's teachings. As we praise his name in music, may we rededicate ourselves to Thee. Help us to become more worthy of the devotions of our families and of the heritage of this nation. As, nursed by nature, trees bud and flowers smile, so, nurtured by the Bible, may we grow into Christ's image, in whose name we pray. Amen.

* * * *

Guest Speaker

Blessed be Thou, O Lord, for Thou hast created order out of chaos, and paved the way of salvation from a sinner to a saint. Bless our speaker according to Thy will, and enable us to embrace the doctrine of the Christ. In our savior's name we pray. Amen.

Note: "Doctrine" means teaching.

Ministerial Conference

Come Thou, blessed Lord. With Thy omnipresent mercy look upon this assembly of Thy ministers. With Thy omniscient grace hear our prayers of adoration, thanksgiving, confession and supplication. With Thy omnipotent wisdom guide and direct the course of this gathering. With Thy unfailing compassion wilt Thou accept our sacrifices of rededication and reconsecration to the cause of Jesus the Christ, and let Thy will be done on earth even as it is in heaven. In our savior's name· Amen.

Note: Any servant of God is a minister. An elder is certainly a minister in this sense.

* * * * *

Missionary Conference

O Lord, mighty and merciful. It was Thy potent word that turned back the sea of reeds. It was Thy potent word that withheld the waters of the Jordan. It was Thy potent word that has become flesh in the savior of mankind. We thank Thee for the mystery of the power of Thy grace which turns sinners into saints, which propels believers unto nonbelievers, and which gives victory over death· As Thou hast ordered the universe to be and to become, so may Thy gospel order the lives of all children of man. Instill within us that potency and that mystery of active peace which Thou alone canst give. Through Jesus Christ, our lord. Amen.

Note: The Red Sea is called "sea of reeds" in the Hebrew Bible. As God created the universe by His word, so by His incarnate word He creates a saint out of a sinner. "Peace" in the Bible has a much more active sense than in English.

15

Our Father, mighty and merciful, humbly do we bow before Thee at the beginning of this another session of our gathering, and thank Thee for the saving grace and redeeming mercy of the Christ. We thank Thee for the simplicity of rural life, and its relation to the simplicity of New Testament Christianity. Help us to realize the significance of Thy house in maintaining our ideals and expanding Thy kingdom. May Thy tabernacle be exalted above all that which is good, true and beautiful in the mundane world. In Jesus' name we pray. Amen.

Scriptures: II Samuel 7:1-11; Haggai 1:2-8.

Note: To a total stranger, who travels through this blessed land, two distinct welcome signs are the towering steeple of the church and the imposing belfry of the school, especially in the rural area. Alas, these signs gradually disapear, when a city grows!

Praised be Thou, O Lord, for Thy word incarnate, in whom we live, move, and have our being. We thank Thee for this dawn of another day in the chronicle of this Thy own congregation. May the foundation of Thy new house of worship be a veritable rock of salvation· May the rise of Thy new house of prayer declare the glory of Thy handiwork. May the ministry of Thy new house of assembly become the fountain of living water to the saints and sages of tomorrow. We rededicate ourselves to Thy cause, O Lord. With Thy abundant mercy bless us, as Thou wilt. In our savior's name we pray. Amen.

Note: Acts 17:28 says in part: ". . . in him we live and move, and have our being. . . ." The house of worship is often called "house of prayer" or "house of assembly" in Judeo-Christian literature. In Hebrew and Greek, the word for "house" sometimes means family or household.

Dedication of New Unit

Come Thou, almighty God. Look down upon the handiwork of Thy children. Amid the threats of impending war and the despair of the suffering righteous throughout the world, we acknowledge Thy providence that has placed us in this blessed land of liberty. In gratitude, do we dedicate to Thee these humble fruits of our labor; and thank Thee for the devoted thought, consecrated skill, and contributed material that have enabled us to magnify this Thy house of worship. May through the portals of this new unit Thy shepherds guide the flock to the fountain of living water. May within the portals of the new chapel the divine peace of sweet communion dispel the darkness of earthly faults. O Lord, in utmost humility do we place ourselves in Thy hands as a living sacrifice. May the deathless cross shine through us unto the uttermost parts of Thy creation. In our savior's name we pray. Amen.

* * * * *

Dinner

Word — Wisdom

Praised be Thou, O Lord, for Thy love and mercy gathered us together about these tables. We thank Thee for Thy word incarnate, who speaks unto us here tonight, as he spake along the shores of Galilee. We thank Thee for Thy divine wisdom which speaks unto us tonight, as she spake in the streets of Jerusalem. Let us hear Thy word. Let us listen to Thy wisdom whisper. Bless the food and this fellowship according to Thy will, and make us Thine, now and forevermore. Amen.

Scriptures: Proverb 8:1-4; Mark 1:14-28; John 1:14.

18

Dinner

Promotion

O Lord, because of our consciousness of Thy presence, we bow before Thee. Because of our feeling of Thy assured guidance, we thank Thee. Because of the awareness of our weakness, we beseech Thee. We thank Thee because of the constant growth of this Thy house of worship. We beseech Thee because of the plans that lie before us. May this blessed Christian fellowship now about these tables be not in vain· May we receive a positive command, as we listen to our distinguished speaker tonight. May we make ourselves vitally useful for the cause of the Christ, to whom be glory forever and ever. Amen.

Note: "House of worship" refers to the church building. Some Jewish synagogues bear this name, though the phrase is expressed in Hebrew.

WORSHIP

Invocation

Come Thou, almighty God. The heavens and the earth praise Thee. Command, O God of hosts, as we humbly bow before Thee. By virtue of our trust in Thee, we surrender to Thee our flesh, our blood, yea, our all. Open our spiritual eyes so that we may behold Thy countenance. Open our spiritual ears so that we may hear Thy voice. In our savior's name. Amen.

* * * *

Thanksgiving

Magnified, exalted, and sanctified be Thy name, O Lord God, for Thou hast given us this day of Thanksgiving. As David of ancient Israel, so do we, as sons and daughters of true Israel, even as the disciples of the Christ, assemble here to praise Thy majesty and magnificence. May Thy infinite mercy render this act of worship acceptable in Thy sight. In our savior's name we pray. Amen.

Scripture: II Samuel 7:27-29.

21

Invocation

We wait for Thee, O Lord; may we renew our strength.
We wait for Thee, O Lord; may we rekindle our faith.
We wait for Thee, O Lord; may we behold Thy countenance.
We wait for Thee, O Lord; may we hear Thy voice.
Bless this assembly according to Thy will. Amen.

* * * * *

O Thou rock, shield and redeemer of the righteous, grant, we pray, that we walk in Thy light. Bless this gathering, and enable us to glorify Thy incarnate word. Amen.

Invocation

Come Thou, almighty God. Look down upon the assembly of Thy servants. With contrite spirits, do we approach the golden throne of the Christ. May our rededication be acceptable in Thy sight, O Lord, lord of lords, king of kings. In our savior's name we pray. Amen.

* * * * *

Come Thou, almighty God, Father of mankind. With Thy abundant mercy and ever-present love, look upon this assembly of Thy children. Hear their prayers of confession, their supplications of faith, and their songs of praise. Be with us and bless us according to Thy will, O Lord. We ask through Jesus, the Christ. Amen.

Invocation

Come Thou, blessed Lord. With Thy unfailing mercy look upon this assembly of Thy ministers. Accept their sacrifices of rededication and reconsecration to Thy cause, and let Thy will be done on earth even as it is in heaven. Be with us, O Lord, as we worship Thee. Amen.

> *Note: All servants of God are "ministers." Therefore, all Christians should be ministers.*

* * * *

Come Thou, almighty God. The heavens and the earth praise Thee. Command, O God of hosts, as we humbly bow before Thee. May Thy tabernacle be exalted upon the holy hill, may Thy people walk in Thy divine light, and may Thy kingdom descend upon Thy wondrous creation. Grant us that grace, that faith, and that peace which belong to the shepherd of shepherds, even Jesus Christ. Amen.

General

O Thou, mighty God, merciful God, the Lord of space, the Lord of time, and the Ruler of the world in which we live, we praise Thy name. We thank Thee for the Christ and his church, for his gospel and his ministry, for the saints and sages of the past, and for disciples and ministers of today and tomorrow. With humble hearts and contrite spirits, we confess before Thy throne of glory our faults and transgressions as members of Thy household. But Thou knowest all, O Lord. We rededicate our all to Thee as a living sacrifice. Awake our souls from the scarlet couches of complacency, and cleanse them whiter than snow, and render them purer than the lily of the valley. Put Thy Holy Spirit upon us. Inspire us. Strengthen us when we are weary. Sustain us when we fall. Guard us when we face the forces of evil. But use us according to Thy will. Father, bless Thy church. May all nations flow unto the spiritual hill of Zion. May all peoples follow in the footsteps of our master, even Jesus, the Christ. In his name we pray. Amen.

* * * * *

May Thy name be praised, O Lord. I confess my ignorance as to the nature of the soul's cry of those who have gathered here in Thy presence, but I know that Thou art omniscient. Wilt Thou hearken to their prayers, and bless them according to Thy will. Draw us ever nearer to the Christ, as we worship Thee. In his name we pray. Amen.

Note: "Name" means person in the above prayer.

Pastoral Prayer

General

O Thou, light of the world. From the shadow of our daily burden, humbly do we draw near unto Thy light trusting in Thy mercy unto us. We thank Thee for this peace and for this comfort which flow into our hearts, as we thus communicate with Thee. We place ourselves in Thy hand, and we find ourselves in Thy care. We behold Thy glorious countenance, and we sense Thy grace upon us. We listen to Thy divine voice, and we are healed by Thy love. For this mystery we thank Thee, O Lord. Help us to learn to live near unto Thee, and embrace the beauty of Thy holiness. We ask through Jesus Christ, our Lord. Amen.

Note: As in English, "hand" means power or authority in Greek and Hebrew, in some passages of the Bible.

General

Come Thou, almighty God. The heavens and the earth praise Thee. Command, O God of hosts, as we humbly bow before Thee. By virtue of our trust in Thy promise we now surrender to Thee our flesh, our blood, yea, our all. Wilt Thou bless this assembly of Thy children, and others who were unable to come. May Thy tabernacle be exalted upon Thy holy hill. May Thy people walk in Thy divine light. May Thy kingdom descend upon Thy wondrous creation. Grant, O Lord, to those innocent and courageous throughout the world who suffer today for Thy name's sake, that grace, that faith, and that peace which Thou alone canst give. Through Jesus Christ, our lord. Amen.

* * * * *

Come Thou, almighty God. The cedars of Lebanon praise Thee. The roses of Sharon adore Thee. The heavens and the earth worship Thee. We confess before Thee our steadfast faith in Thy word incarnate, and thank Thee for Thy redeeming love. We pray that Thou wilt watch over these Thy children as they participate in this worship. Bless them, our Father, as they listen to the proclamation of the gospel; and enlighten them with Thy word. With mercy accept their rededication to Thy cause, and recreate others who confess the name of the Christ. Glory be unto Thee, O God, forever and ever. Amen.

Note: "Gospel" means good news.

Pastoral Prayer

General

O Thou, creator of the universe and Father of mankind, we thank Thee for these precious moments of prayer when we may communicate with Thee. Hear our humble words of adoration, confession, thanksgiving and supplication. May our thoughts be cleansed, may our words be purified, and may our deeds become acceptable in Thy sight. Draw us nearer to the perfect image of the Christ. In his name we pray. Amen.

* * * * *

Almighty God, Father of our good shepherd, even Jesus Christ. May Thy name be praised for this communion of the saints. We confess our steadfast faith in that good shepherd, who leaves the ninety-nine to seek the one that is lost. Bless all members of Thy holy household, those who are in Thy presence here, and others who are absent. Like rain unto parched land, may Thy grace renew our lives; like water unto thirsty souls, may Thy love heal our sorrows; like bread unto hungry persons, may Thy mercy sustain our faith. Let the beam of Thy shining cross penetrate our hearts, and let us truly feel the warmth of its glow. To that ancient cross be glory forever and ever. Amen.

Note: The simile of the good shepherd appears in Matthew 18:12-14; Luke 15:4-7.

Pastoral Prayer

General

O Lord, our Lord, Lord of all mankind, we thank Thee for our glorious consciousness of Thy presence in the temporal darkness of human turmoil. Towering above the mundane chaos of vanities and transgressions, let there arise within us Christian faith, hope and love. Bless this Thy church, its minister, his family, its officers, their families, its other members, their families, and those other members of Thy household here and abroad. Be with us as we worship Thee, and grant us that silent power of truth that has become flesh in Jesus Christ, in whose name we pray. Amen.

* * * * *

Praised be Thou, O Lord, creator of the universe and Father of mankind. In these precious moments of prayer, humbly do we approach Thy golden throne of grace; and we thank Thee for this hour of worship and for the ministry of the Christ. Wilt Thou dispel our rebellious thoughts and stubborn minds; and let us sense and acknowledge here and now something greater than the sacrifice of sheep and oxen, something greater than the temple of Zion, and something greater than even the law of Moses, for Christ died for us. As the new creation of the Christ, let us each bear the marks of his salvation. As we bless Thy name, so wilt Thou bless those who hearken to the gospel proclaimed. Lead us on, O king eternal. Let us walk in Thy light. In Jesus' name we pray. Amen.

Pastoral Prayer

General

Praised be Thou, O Lord, creator of the universe, who hast made man in Thy own image and likeness. We thank Thee for these golden moments of prayer, when we speak to Thee, and when we may hear Thy voice. We thank Thee for Thy precious gift to us, even Jesus Christ. We confess and confirm our steadfast faith in him. Bless those who worship Thee according to Thy will, and accept the sacrifice of those who rededicate themselves to Thy cause. Wilt Thou guard and guide those who are absent, heal and comfort those who are sick, and strengthen and console those who are bereaved. Implant in our hearts the ancient cross, and let us embrace that peace which Thou alone canst give. In Jesus' name. Amen.

Note: Genesis 1:26 says in part: ". . . Let us make man in our image, after our likeness. . . ." The Hebrew word for "image" may signify the external form, and that for "likeness" the internal relation.

Minister

O Lord, our Lord, creator of the universe, and Father of mankind. We praise Thy name. We thank Thee for these golden moments of Christian life when we may communicate with Thee, and for Thy providence that has brought us to this Thy house of worship. With humble hearts and contrite spirits, do we confess our steadfast faith in Thy only begotten son. As we meditate on Thy holy word, enable us to be just and righteous, honest and kind, and virtuous and pious. When we fall sustain us. When we fail encourage us. When we are weak strengthen us. We ask Thy blessings upon this congregation and its minister, and upon all churches of the world and their ministers. With mercy look upon these Thy children, as they bear the burden of the cross. To that ancient cross be glory and majesty, forever and ever. Amen.

Pastoral Prayer

Minister

Humbly do we bow before Thee at the beginning of this hour of worship, and thank Thee for Thy breath that has made us living souls· Acknowledging Thy command to rule over Thy creation as Thy sons and daughters, we pray that Thou wilt help us to cultivate that faith which has been rooted in the rock of salvation. May that faith withstand the crushing waves of temporal evil and the dashing surge of mundane chaos. Wilt Thou bless our distinguished speaker, and make us proper receptacles for his message. In our savior's name. Amen.

> *Note: Genesis 2:7 says in part: "... God ... breathed into his nostrils the breath of life, and man became a living soul." Genesis 1:28 says in part: "... God said ... fill the earth and subdue it, and have dominion over ... every living thing. ..." The phrase "rock of my salvation" is found in Psalms 89:26, and "rock of our salvation" in Psalms 95:1. "... And that rock was Christ," says I Corinthians 10:4.*

Pastoral Prayer

Minister

O God, God of all mankind, humbly do we bring ourselves to Thee at the beginning of this hour of worship, and thank Thee for Thy providence that has placed us in this land of liberty and peace. Help us to be just and honest, enable us to be kind and gracious, and may we be virtuous and pious, to the end that we may become more worthy of the membership in Thy church. We ask Thy blessings upon our guest minister who has come to us to proclaim Thy good news. We ask Thy blessing upon our own minister and other ministers who are gathered in. . . . May they stay on Thy side today and forever, so that the cross of our savior may be glorified. We ask this, together with our earnest supplication for Thy mercy upon the innocent suffering now throughout the world, in Jesus' name. Amen.

Note: "Gospel" means the good news. This prayer was used in the absence of the minister who was attending a Christian convention in a faraway city.

mankind. We thank Thee for Thy gracious providence that has brought us together to worship Thee, for Christ's tender ministry that has given us Thy peace, and for these golden moments of prayer when we may communicate with Thee. Bless all who speak unto Thee, according to Thy will. Open our ears and let us hear Thy voice. Open our eyes and let us behold Thy countenance. And through this mystic communion let us realize the power of prayer. Grant to our minister that courage, that wisdom, and that insight, which Thou alone canst give, as he speaks unto us. To the ancient cross be glory forever and ever. Amen.

* * * * *

Praised be Thy name, O Lord of the universe and Father of mankind. We thank Thee for Thy steadfast love that has brought us together to worship Thee. As we humbly approach Thy golden throne of holiness, hear our prayers of confession and supplication. Bless this Thy congregation according to Thy will, especially our minister and his family, and our guests and visitors in Thy presence. May Thy guiding spirit rest upon our guest minister, and make him speak Thy word. Grant us all that faith and courage, with which to press on towards the higher goal of life. Through Jesus Christ, our Lord. Amen.

> *Note: "Steadfast love" is one recent translation of the Hebrew word, which was frequently rendered "mercy." Neither translation gives the profound meaning of this word. "Religious love" or "religous mercy" may give a better sense.*

34

Minister

Come Thou, almighty God, God of the universe and Father of mankind. With Thy abundant grace look upon this assembly of Thy children. Wilt Thou accept our heartfelt praise and humble thanksgiving, and hear our sincere confession and earnest supplication. Bless, O Lord, each person present here. Bless our minister and his family, and bless our visiting minister for this service. May Thy guiding, sustaining, comforting, and healing hand be upon all believers, and enable them to share that peace which Thou alone canst give. Glory be to Thy throne and to the ancient cross. Through Jesus Christ, our savior, we pray. Amen.

* * * * *

Nature

Lord of the universe and Father of mankind, for the renewal of life within Thy own creation, and for the conquest of death by Thy holy son, we thank Thee. Let us truly worship Thee with heartfelt confession and thanksgiving. With utmost joy and steadfast peace, may our souls soar like the birds of heaven, may our hearts blossom like the lilies of the field, and may our song of praise rise unto Thee like the sweet incense of old. Let us hear Thy word proclaimed, O God. There is none beside Thee. In Jesus' name we pray. Amen.

Pastoral Prayer

Spring

Once again do we humbly bow before Thee, O Lord, confessing our faith in Thy word incarnate. We thank Thee for the cross, symbol of sacrifice and salvation. We thank Thee for Thy love, token of purity and perfection. May the songs of birds and the smiles of flowers enhance our devotion to the cause, for which the Christ was sent to mankind. Let us rededicate ourselves to Thee for that cause, as we truly listen to the proclamation of the gospel of the Christ, in whose name we pray. Amen.

* * * * *

Autumn — Unity

Magnified and exalted be Thy name, O God of the universe and Father of mankind. With utmost faith in Thy only begotten son, do we assemble here to worship Thee. We thank Thee for the many and varied gifts of Thy holy spirit. Though we are not alike in talents, abilities and occupations, help us to realize the oneness of Thy church. Like colorful autumnal leaves let us be woven into the unity of the golden brocade of Thy household, each contributing much to its beautiful unity. Let us love one another as Thy children, and may Thy peace reign over us now and forevermore. Amen.

Pastoral Prayer

Autumn

Glory be unto Thee, O Father of all mankind, for the shining heavenly stars above, for the colorful autumnal leaves below, for the innocent sleep of a babe, for the vigorous activities of the youth, and for the quiet repose of the aged. Grant us the spiritual insight that we may discern Thy potent wisdom which manifests itself in every sphere of the universe. May that divine wisdom guide us throughout this assembly, and may we truly sense Thy presence among us. To this end, and to the end that the ministry of the Christ be established and exalted, do we invoke Thy blessing upon us. Hear us now, as we pray in the words of our blessed Lord: Our father in heaven, hallowed be Thy name. Thy kingdom come. Thy will be done on earth as it is in heaven. Give us this day our daily bread, and forgive us our debts as we forgive our debtors. Lead us not into temptation, but deliver us from evil. For Thine is the kingdom, and the power, and the glory. Forever and ever. Amen.

Note: The doxology of the Lord's prayer is not found in the leading manuscripts of the New Testament.

Winter

Magnified and exalted be Thy name, our heavenly Father, for Thou hast brought us together to worship Thee. We thank Thee for the unfathomable power which Thou hast enshrined in the universe, and for the wondrous virtue which Thou hast bestowed upon man through Jesus Christ. Yet we confess that from time to time we have gone astray, we have stumbled, we have forgotten our mission and ministry, and thus we have sinned. Lord, cleanse us again as we submit ourselves to Thee. So let us serve Thee by serving Thy children, and let us prepare the way for the advent of the Christ. Though the snow and ice encompass us without, let Thy love and grace warm our hearts within. Be merciful unto those who suffer this day mentally or physically, and let Thy peace prevail over us, world without end. In Jesus' name we pray. Amen.

Note: "Name" signifies person. In Judaism "The Name" means God.

Christmas

Our Father in heaven, we thank Thee for the glowing star of ancient Bethlehem. We thank Thee for the silent power of Thy ordered universe. We thank Thee for Thy holy love of Thy Christ Jesus. May the golden brocade with a woof of silent power and a warp of holy love be woven within our conscience, and may that golden brocade impel us to find joy in sharing pain, hunger, distress and despair of all mankind. Wilt Thou nourish the unfailing virtues of Christian manhood and womanhood to the end that we may at last manifest that silent power and holy love which have become flesh in Thy only begotten son. Amen.

* * * * *

O creator of the universe, for the sun of Thy glory over Jerusalem, for the moon of Thy wisdom over Carmel, and for the star of Thy intelligence over Bethlehem, we thank Thee. As we participate in this worship, may it be the star of hope that leads us to Thy perfect peace. Let it prevail over us, O Lord. Let Thy peace prevail over mankind now and evermore. Amen.

Note: "Peace" in the Bible means, not only the cessation of war, but also safety, healthiness, completeness, etc.

Pastoral Prayer

New Year

Our gracious Father, who hast ordained seasons and years, and who hast created man in Thy own image, we most humbly bow before Thee at the beginning of this new year with the sense of seriousness of the commission that Thou hast given to us to bear the ark of the New Testament even unto the uttermost parts of the world that Thou hast prepared for us. With shame do we look upon the days gone by, for we were not ready and caused Thee to "break out upon us;" but now we are determined to carry on with renewed faith, hope and love. Awaken our consciousness to the fact that we are living souls. Create in us the perception of Christian duties and responsibilities. Enable us to sanctify ourselves to Thee and Thy only son, to whom be glory forever and ever. Amen.

Scripture: I Chronicles 15:12-15; Matthew 28:18-20.

Lord's Table

General

O Lord, let the heavens sing and the earth rejoice, for Thou hast given us Jesus the Christ. We thank Thee for the ancient cross signifying the Christ's conquest over death, and for this holy emblem confirming our trust in Thy saving grace. As we participate in this sacred feast, let there arise within us a renewed sense of faith, hope and love. May Thy counsel endure from the rising of the sun even unto its setting. Glory be to the Christ, in whose name we pray. Amen.

* * * * *

Mighty God and merciful Father, we thank Thee for this renewal of our precious covenant with Thee, and for this reaffirmation of our victorious faith in the Christ. Enable us to surrender ourselves unto Thee, that we might gain the spiritual power with which to resist evil, and the divine wisdom with which to practice righteousness. Let us remember Thee every moment in holy anticipation of the life eternal. Through Jesus Christ, our lord. Amen.

Lord's Table

General

Praised be Thou, O Lord, for Thou art the healer, comforter, sustainer, and savior of all mankind. We thank Thee for Thy exceeding mercy which enables us to participate in this feast of the New Covenant· As we partake of this emblem, let every element of our existence rejoin in this divine mystery, let every fibre of our being respond to Thy call, and let our hearts and minds indeed find refuge in Thy word incarnate. To him be glory forever and ever. Amen.

> *Note: The Greek word for disposition, will or testament is often translated "covenant" in the English New Testament. The primary meaning of the Hebrew word translated "covenant" is an agreement between two parties, e.g. between God and Israel.*

* * * * *

Mighty God, merciful Father, we thank Thee for this communion with Thee, for this communion of the Christ, and for this communion with the saints. As Thou hast given the Christ unto us, so let us give ourselves unto Thee. As Jesus died in our behalf, so let us lay down our lives for Thy cause· Enable us to share the burden of the cross in Christian love and peace, to the end that we may rise again in the newness of life. In his name we pray. Amen.

> *Note: Early Christians were sometimes called "saints" in the New Testament.*

General

Heavenly Father, let us flee for these few moments from the troubled world, so that we may again embrace the vision of the cross. We seek not the way of escape, but we do seek the faith and courage with which to face the tasks and duties before us. May we truly sense Thy presence, as we partake in this sacred feast. In our savior's name. Amen.

*   *   *   *   *

God of mercy, God of love, we thank Thee for these precious moments when we may recapture the ultimate glory of our faith in Christ Jesus. May this sacred emblem instill within us hearts, minds and attitudes as clean as the blue sky and as pure as the white clouds. May Thy golden throne in heaven cast its beauty upon our lives here on earth. In our savior's name. Amen.

Lord's Table

General

Glory be unto Thee, O Lord, for Thou hast given us Christ Jesus, the great shepherd of the sheep. We thank Thee for this reenactment of his memorable feast. As the ancient cross signifies his victory over death, so may our partaking of this blessed emblem mean our sharing in the life eternal. We yield ourselves unto Thee, in order that we may find ourselves in Thy care. We look up unto Thee, in order that we may sense Thy grace. We incline our ears unto Thee, in order that we may hear Thy voice. May the beauty of Thy holiness prevail in our hearts now and forevermore. Amen.

* * * *

O Lord, Lord of the universe, our Lord, there is none beside Thee. We thank Thee for Thy word incarnate, even Jesus Christ. In memory of his victorious deed and saving grace, do we participate in this feast. May the ancient cross illumine our souls. May this sacred emblem warm our hearts. May we truly rejoin the fold of Thy sheep. Grant us peace. We pray in Jesus' name. Amen.

Lord's Table

General

O Thou, Lord of mercy, Lord of grace, we thank Thee for Thy own image in Jesus Christ, and for this token of his redeeming love. May this reenactment of his Last Supper signify the reaffirmation of our faith in him. May this renewal of the New Covenant mean the reawakening of our souls. May our realization of Thy omnipresence denote the revitalization of our Christian fellowship. Let Thy rod and Thy staff sustain us, as we walk humbly in the footsteps of our master, and let the ancient cross illumine our hearts now and forevermore. In our savior's name we pray. Amen.

> *Note: "New Covenant" of II Corinthians 3:14 is rendered "New Testament" in the Authorized Version (King James Version) of 1611. "Rod" and "staff" appear in Psalm 23:4. The Hebrew word for "rod" means a club, and that for "staff" a stick used for supporting oneself.*

* * * * *

Praised be Thou, O Lord, for Christ's victory over death, for his gift of the New Covenant, and for his saving grace unto all mankind. With thankful hearts and contrite spirits, do we partake of this holy emblem, and we pray that this our act of participation in the enactment of his memorial feast will truly render that which is temporal to permanent, that which is perishable to imperishable, and that which is mortal to immortal. May the power of Thy mystery manifest itself in our hearts, now and evermore. Amen.

Lord's Table

General

Blessed be Thou, O Lord, creator of the universe and redeemer of mankind. We thank Thee for the divine victory over death, and for the human urge for perfection. As we partake of this heavenly emblem, may that which is divine and that which is human unite by Thy grace. And may that unity blossom into the flower of eternal peace which Thou alone canst give. In our savior's name we pray. Amen.

* * * * *

Our heavenly Father, we thank Thee for these precious moments of Thy grace which has brought us to this table of the New Covenant. As we partake of this sacred emblem, may it truly remold our souls. Let it supplant our doubt with faith, despair with hope, ill will with love, and strife with peace. May Thy guiding star ever illumine the pathway of life, now and forevermore. Amen.

Almighty God, who hast filled the heavens above with Thy glory, and the earth below with Thy love, we praise Thy name. We thank Thee for Thy beauty that our spiritual eyes behold, and for Thy voice that our discerning ears hear. Above all, do we thank Thee for Thy word that has become flesh, and for our vision of his cross. Grant us faith and strength, with which to exalt and magnify our blessed savior, as we humbly partake in this feast of the New Covenant. Guide us, O Lord, through the path of peace. In Jesus' name. Amen.

* * * *

Father of mankind. If ever our faith wavers, if ever our hope fails, and if ever our love wanes, let us reconsecrate ourselves at this feast. Wilt Thou nourish the best of men. Wilt Thou save the worst of men. May the towering cross stand forever, the eternal beacon lighting the way of life to the Christ. In his name we pray. Amen.

Lord's Table

General

For the wonders of Thy creation, for the love of Thy Christ, and for the faith of Thy people, we thank Thee. As we partake of this feast of the New Covenant, make us again prisoners of Thy cross. May the bonds of Christ's love eat into our flesh. May the chains of our faith bore into our souls. May we, within these bonds and chains, find eternal freedom and peace. In our savior's name. Amen.

* * * * *

Praised be Thou, O Lord, for Thou art omnipresent, omnipotent and omniscient. We thank Thee for Thy word incarnate, even Jesus Christ. Bless this emblem which is about to nourish our faith in his victory over death. May this holy communion sustain us, though mountains fall upon us, though floods sweep over us, and though the forces of evil surround us. We pray in Jesus' name. Amen.

Note: "Omnipresent" means present in all places; "omnipotent," all-powerful; and "omniscient," knowing all things.

Lord's Table

General

Blessed be Thou, O Lord, for the crown of Thy creation, even Jesus Christ. With humble hearts and contrite spirits, do we commemorate his supreme sacrifice. May the vision of the ancient cross rise before us. May that vision remain in our hearts. May that vision nourish our faith. May that vision sustain our lives, though we walk in the shadow of death. Through Jesus Christ, our lord. Amen.

* * * * *

Our Father, Thou hast spoken, and the universe came to order. Thou hast spoken, and the Christ came to save. Thou hast spoken, and we come to participate in this sacred feast. May this precious emblem engender in our hearts the still small voice of courage, faith, hope and love. In our savior's name· Amen.

Lord's Table

General

O Lord, in whom we live, move and have our being, we come to Thee trusting in Thy mercy unto us. As dew unto withered flower and rain unto parched land, so may this emblem revive our weary souls. As we rededicate ourselves to Thee at this Thy own table of the New Covenant, may Thy watchful providence sustain us in the days to come. In comfort, may we not forget Thee. In suffering, let us remember Thy everlasting love. In Jesus' name we pray. Amen.

Note: Generally speaking, "New Covenant" is understood to mean the New Testament. See II Corinthians 3:14, King James Version. "Covenant" signifies agreement, rather than testifying.

* * * * *

O Thou, Lord, God of mercy and God of love, we thank Thee for Thy creative power of life and resurrection. In order that we may celebrate Christ's victory over death, humbly do we partake of this heavenly emblem. Cleanse us, remold us, and remake us according to Thy will, so that at last we may share in the glory of Thy only begotten son. In his name we pray. Amen.

Lord's Table

General

O Thou, creator of the perfect image of man, we thank Thee for this feast of the New Covenant. As we partake of this heavenly emblem, help us to face with grace all problems of life, to return good for evil, and to love those who hate us. Let Thy peace reign over us, like the silvery moon over the shepherd's tent. In our savior's name, we pray· Amen.

Note: "New Covenant" is translated "New Testament" in II Corinthians 3:14, King James Version. "Covenant" is preferable.

* * * *

Glory be to Thee, O God, omnipotent, omniscient and omnipresent. We thank Thee for this precious table of the New Covenant. With mercy look upon the observance of Thy own ordinance. With grace lead us to the ancient cross. As we partake of this blessed emblem, may bruised lives be healed, may crushed hearts be lifted, and may burdened souls be strengthened. In our savior's name. Amen.

Note: "Omnipotent" means all-powerful, "omniscient," knowing all things, and "omnipresent," present in all places· Many Christians, Disciples, regard the Lord's Supper as an "ordinance" rather than a "sacrament." "New Covenant" is referred to in some texts of the Dead Sea Scrolls. See also Jeremiah 31:31.

51

Lord's Table

General

Our heavenly Father, we thank Thee for the revelation of Thy will in this precious ordinance. Though our earthly knowledge fails to comprehend the mystery of the manifestation of Thy love, by faith do we believe in Thy saving grace, and in trust do we partake of this emblem. Help us to enter truly into the fellowship of our Lord's suffering. Enable us to find therein that perfect peace which he alone can give. Amen.

* * * * *

Blessed be Thou, O Lord, Father of mankind. From the earthly dust to the living soul, and from the living soul to the immortal life, Thou hast paved the way of the truth. In order that we may ever remember the priceless debt we owe to the Christ, do we humbly partake in this heavenly feast. Grant us, O God, adequate strength, saintly courage, and sufficient faith, which may ever kindle our hope for that true, beautiful and good peace, which Thou alone canst give. Amen.

Scriptures: Genesis 2:7, 19; Romans 2:7; II Timothy 1:10; John 14:27; Philippians 4:7.

Lord's Table

General

Wonderful Lord, precious Lord, we thank Thee for Thy only begotten son. In memory of his supreme sacrifice, do we humbly partake of this feast. Grant, O Lord, that our hands be empowered for the service of our fellowmen, that our shoulders be strengthened for sharing the burden of our neighbors, and that our faith be fortified for the edification of our friends. Let us find joy and peace in our wholehearted devotion to the cause for which Jesus died for us. In his name we pray. Amen·

* * * * *

O Thou, God of light, God of love, we thank Thee for this precious privilege to approach Thee in partaking of the feast of Thy own. Bless us according to Thy will. Cleanse us of our faults and transgressions. Enable us to envision, embrace and enhance the power of the cross upon which Jesus died for us. In his name we pray. Amen.

Father of mankind, for the ever-present glow of our faith in the cross, we thank Thee. May it be with utmost humility that we partake of this heavenly feast. May it be with wholehearted devotion that we rededicate ourselves to Thy cause. May it be with complete confidence that we henceforth walk in Thy light. Through Jesus Christ we pray. Amen.

* * * * *

O Lord, our Lord, how excellent is Thy name. We thank Thee for the crown of Thy creation, even Jesus Christ. In memory of his precious life of sacrifice, do we partake of this blessed emblem. May the rock of Thy salvation withstand the dashing surge of human sorrows, disappointments and temptations. To the cross of Calvary be glory forever and ever. Amen.

For Thy many mercies and endless grace, do we lift up our hearts unto Thee in gratitude. As we partake of this emblem, may our conscience be reborn, may our lives be renewed, and may our homes be rebuilt upon the rock of Thy salvation. We abide in Thee, O Great Spirit. Abide in us forevermore. Amen.

* * * * *

Our Father, we thank Thee for this feast of Thy heavenly love. As we participate in this holy ordinance, let us share the heavy burden Jesus once bore. Guide us along the shadowy path when we stagger. Show us the radiant cross when we are crushed. Lead us in the rocky path where the Christ trod. In his name we pray. Amen.

Lord's Table

General

We thank Thee, O Lord, for this symbol of Thy redeeming love.
With contrite spirits, do we partake in this ordinance. May the
ancient cross sustain our faith. May that faith be the burning fire
that consumes the power of evil. May that faith be the golden
sunshine that yields joy to the world. May that faith be the silvery
moonlight that gives us eternal peace. To the prince of that peace
be glory and honor forever and ever. Amen.

*   *   *   *   *

We thank Thee, our heavenly Father, for Thy ever-unfailing love
unto us. By virtue of that love, we approach Thee now in this
sacred ordinance of our lord. By the New Covenant in his blood,
may we confirm our Christian faith. Through the cross of Calvary,
may we rededicate ourselves to our master. Enable us at last to
live, move and have our being in him, who is our savior and
redeemer. Amen.

Scripture: Acts 17:28.

*Note: Many Christians, Disciples, prefer "ordinance" to
"sacrament." "Covenant" signifies solemn agreement.
"New Covenant" refers to Christian agreement with God.*

Lord's Table

General

Our heavenly Father, we thank Thee for the power of Thy New Covenant that has gathered us beneath one cross. As there is one Lord for all mankind, so may all peoples be one. As there is one table for Thy supper, so may all Christians be one. Let the principle of sacrifice be manifest throughout Thy creation. In Jesus' name. Amen.

Scripture: Ephesians 4:4-6.

Note: "Covenant" means solemn agreement. The Greek word for it is sometimes translated "testament." See, for example, Mark 14:24; II Corinthians 3:6, etc., in King James Version. Later English versions render it "covenant."

* * * * *

Most humbly do we approach Thee, our heavenly Father, as we participate in this sacred ordinance. We thank Thee for the cross. We acknowledge Thy love. And we believe in Thy only son. As he gave his precious life for us, so do we submit our lives to Thee a living sacrifice. May they be acceptable to Thee for the upbuilding of Thy kingdom. In our savior's name we pray. Amen.

Note: "Ordinance" means an authoritative command. It resulted, in this case, in the Lord's Supper. "Thy only begotten son" is familiar to older Christian people. "Thy only son" is sufficient, as in more recent English versions.

Lord's Table

General

Our redeemer liveth, O Lord. We thank Thee for his life, his death and his resurrection. In memory of his precious sacrifice, do we partake of this divine feast. May the golden portals of eternal life be opened, and may we behold the jeweled crown of his everlasting glory. In Jesus' name we pray. Amen.

Note: Job 19:25 says: "For I know that my redeemer lives. . . ."

* * * * *

O Lord, let Christian zeal permeate our throbbing hearts, as we partake of this feast of the New Covenant. May every drop of our sinful blood receive the redeeming blood of the Christ. May every morsel of our earthly flesh accept the heavenly flesh of our savior. May our whole person thus become a living example of the cross. Through Jesus Christ, our lord. Amen.

Note: "New Covenant" means Christian agreement with God. "Cross" in this prayer signifies the symbol of the crucifixion of Jesus, or the symbol of the Christian faith.

Lord's Table

General

May Thy name be praised, O God of all mankind. We thank Thee for this our experience of Thy presence among us. May this experience remove all stains of our thoughts, and render them as clean as the waters of the Jordan. May it erase all faults of our lives, and make them as pure as the snow upon Mt. Hermon. May our self-dedication to Thy cause be acceptable in Thy sight, O Lord, our savior and our redeemer. In Christ's name. Amen.

Note: The water of the Jordan is not always clean, but rather muddy during the rainy season, especially as it pours into the Salt Sea, commonly called the Dead Sea.

* * * * *

O Thou, master workman of the universe, in the crimson sky of the morn, in the violet heaven of the eventide, day after day, and night after night the wonder of Thy wisdom surges within us. We thank Thee for this sanctified emblem. As we partake in this holy feast, we pray that we might truly enter into the fellowship of the suffering of our blessed Lord. To his eternal cross be glory forever and ever. Amen.

Note: "Sanctified" means to be made holy. That which has been sanctified may produce spiritual blessing.

59

Lord's Table

General

Glory be unto Thee, O Lord of hosts, for Thou hast given the Christ to all mankind. We thank Thee, O God of mercy, for the Christ died for us. With humble hearts and contrite spirits do we partake of this blessed emblem. We pray that we may feel within us the surging power of Thy redeeming love. Let it supplant fear with courage, doubt with trust, and disbelief with faith. Enable us to walk this day in Thy light. Through Jesus Christ, our lord. Amen.

> *Note: The phrase "Lord of hosts" or "Jehovah of hosts" or "Yahweh of hosts" signifies God of army. Sometimes the hosts are identified with the children of Israel, as in Exodus 12:41. One primary meaning of the Hebrew word translated "host" in this phrase is service. So the children of Israel were to serve God, as soldiers do their commander.*

* * * * *

We thank Thee, O Lord, for this wondrous table of Thy own appointment. As we partake of this heavenly emblem, let our eyes behold the risen Christ, let our ears hear his voice, let our mouths sing his praise, let our hearts rejoice in his promise, and let our minds rest in peace. Glory be to Thee and to his cross, this day and forevermore. Amen.

Lord's Table

General

O Lord, our Lord, how glorious and magnificent is Thy name, for Thou hast revealed Thyself in Christ Jesus, and opened our vista unto eternal life. We thank Thee for Thy steadfast love which has brought us to this blessed table of the New Covenant. As we partake of this heavenly emblem, help us to embrace the mystery of Christ's conquest over death. May Thy spirit enter our souls, and let us feel the beauty of Thy holiness. In our savior's name we pray· Amen.

> *Note: "Steadfast love" in this prayer is the highest and noblest religious love, such as the love in Micah 6:8 (translated "mercy" or "kindness" in some English versions), and the love in I Corinthians 13:13. There are several words for love in Hebrew and in Greek.*

* * * * *

Blessed Lord, Father of mankind, with humble hearts and contrite spirits, do we speak unto Thee, trusting in Thy mercy unto us. We thank Thee for this table of the New Covenant, and for this emblem of Thy grace. As we partake of it, let us remember that our own lives were recreated in Thy image by the suffering of Thy own begotten son. Henceforth, may our thoughts be pure, may our words be righteous, and may our lives be blameless. Enable us to share the divine glory of Thy peace with all members of Thy household. In Jesus' name we pray. Amen.

> *Note: "New Covenant" means new agreement with God, that is, Christian agreement compared to Jewish agreement, which is the old covenant. "Begotten" of "Thy own begotten son" may be rightly omitted.*

61

Lord's Table

General

O Thou, Lord of the universe and Father of mankind, we thank Thee for this holy emblem. As we partake of it, once again do we surrender ourselves to Thy care. As the suffering of the Christ forespoke his victory over death, and as the passing of the autumn bespeaks the coming of the spring, so may this renewal of the New Covenant foreshadow for us thoughts that are clean, words that are pure and lives that are perfect. Glory be to the crown of the Christ, now and forevermore. Amen.

> *Note: "New Covenant" here signifies Christian agreement with God; that is, one's confession of faith in Jesus as the Messiah, and one's commitment to his cause.*

* * * * *

Glory be unto Thee, O Lord of the universe and Father of mankind. We thank Thee for this table of the New Covenant. With grateful hearts and utmost humility do we partake of this emblem. Fortify us with Thy mighty word, purify us with Thy holy spirit, and sanctify us with Thy merciful command, to the end that each one of us may have a portion in the kingdom of heaven. Through Jesus Christ we pray. Amen.

> *Note: "New Covenant" is Christian agreement with God. "Covenant" is agreement, rather than testimony. The liturgical reading of each section of the famous Talmudic ethical treatise, called Abot, begins with "All Israel has a portion in the world to come. . . ."*

Lord's Table

General

Our heavenly Father, Thou art omnipresent, omnipotent and omniscient. We praise Thy name. We thank Thee for the benefaction of Thy grace, and for this table of the New Covenant. As we partake of this blessed emblem, draw us ever closer unto Thee. May the shining star over Bethlehem rekindle our hearts, may the ancient cross upon Calvary enlighten our souls, and may we humbly follow in the steps of our master and savior. To this end grant us peace. For Thy name's sake, we pray. Amen.

> *Note: "Name" in "For Thy name's sake" above signifies person, as a personal name means a man or woman who bears it.*

* * * * *

Our Father in heaven, in these moments of quietude bathed in the ray of Thy redeeming grace, we thank Thee for this holy emblem. As we humbly partake of it, let it speak to us of Christ's victory over death. Enable us to offer to Thee our daily sacrifice of service to Thy cause. May the power of our faith dispel from within our hearts fears, doubts, desires and wants, and fill our souls with courage, trust, devotion and peace. Through Jesus Christ we pray. Amen.

Lord's Table

General

Blessed are we, O Lord, for we are the disciples of Christ. Blessed are we, O Lord, for we partake in this feast. Blessed are we, O Lord, for the Christ died for us. For these blessings we thank Thee. May Thy name be blessed, Thy son be blessed, and Thy church be blessed. For these blessings we pray, through Jesus Christ, our lord. Amen.

Note: "Disciple" means learner, or student. See Matthew 28:19-20.

* * * *

Blessed Lord, master of the universe and Father of mankind, we thank Thee for this table of the New Covenant. In memory of the Christ's victory over death, do we humbly partake of this heavenly emblem. Though mountains fall, floods surround us, and the burdens of life bear upon us, let us ever remember Thy saving grace. Enable us to embrace and embody that peace which Thou alone canst give. Through Jesus Christ, our lord. Amen.

Scripture: John 14:27.

Note: "Peace" in the Bible means not only the absence of war, but also sound health, perfect life and general well-being. The Greek word translated "peace" in the New Testament, unlike the Hebrew word in the Old Testament, refers primarily to the absence of war. Covenant" denotes agreement.

* * * *

Lord's Table

General

Heavenly Father, we thank Thee for Thy word that has become flesh, for the burden of the cross which Thou hast placed upon us, and for this Thy table of the New Covenant. With humble hearts and contrite spirits, do we partake of this emblem. Hear us when we pray, teach us when we ask, guide us when we err, sustain us when we fall. Lead us in the path of light and life towards the perfect image of the Christ. In his name we pray. Amen.

> *Note: "New Covenant" is Christian solemn agreement with God. It connotes sound faith in Jesus and whole-hearted commitment to his cause.*

*   *   *   *   *

O God. For the perfect beauty of Thy creation, and especially for the mystery of Thy saving grace, we thank Thee. With grateful hearts and contrite spirits, do we renew our covenant in this sacred communion. We pray that, if the flower of our tree of life fades, let its fragrance linger for tomorrow; if its leaves fall, let it adorn the world to come; if its branches break, let them sustain Thy house of worship. Wilt Thou implant in our midst that tree of Christian faith and virtues. Through Jesus Christ, our lord. Amen.

Lord's Table

General

Blessed be Thou, O Lord, king of the universe and Father of mankind. We thank Thee for this table of Thy saving grace and redeeming love. As we partake of this holy emblem, may the vision of the cross rise before us. Let it confirm, sustain and strengthen our faith in Christ Jesus; and enable us to hear him say: Your faith made you well. Go in peace. In his name we pray. Amen.

Scriptures: Luke 7:36-50; 8:43-48.

Note: "Go in peace" which appears in these passages is a very common greeting at parting. However, it is appropriate here, especially since "peace" means completeness or healthiness.

* * * * *

O Thou, Lord of eternity, may our prayers of adoration for Thy majesty over the universe and thanksgiving for Thy love symbolized in this emblem be acceptable in Thy sight. As we humbly participate in this sacred feast, wilt Thou enter our hearts and let us think as Thou wouldst have us, and wilt Thou use our lips and let them speak Thy word. May our lives be truly cleansed, renewed and refreshed, to the end that they may indeed reflect the beauty of Thy holiness. In our savior's name we pray. Amen.

Lord's Table

> *Bread*

Come Thou, almighty God. Look with grace upon these Thy children. Inspire them with Thy holy spirit, as they partake of this manna from heaven. May Thy light dawn upon their conscience. Let it kindle their faith in Thy promise. Let it give them rest in their mundane struggle. May Thy peace reign over us, even as it does in heaven. Through Jesus Christ, our lord. Amen.

> *Note: "Manna" is the name of the food miraculously given to the Israelites in the exodus. Exodus 16:31 says: "Then the house of Israel called its name 'man'. . . ." "Man" appears in the Greek and Latin translations of the Bible. "Manna" was probably taken from the Aramaic translation of "man." "Mundane" means worldly.*

* * * * *

Our Father in heaven, hallowed be Thy name. We thank Thee for this institution of the New Covenant, and for this precious food from heaven. As we partake of this emblem, may the vision of the cross rise before us. Help us to realize that this act of our participation symbolizes the remission of our sins by Jesus the Christ. Enable us to abide in Thee with clean hearts, steadfast faith, and eternal peace, both now and forevermore. In Jesus' name we pray. Amen.

> *Note: "Hallowed" means made holy or sacred. "New Covenant" signifies Christian agreement with God.*

Lord's Table

Bread

We thank Thee, O God, for these golden moments of Christian worship. We now behold Thy glorious countenance. We now feel Thy unfailing love. We now live and have our being in Thee. Facing the grim facts and dark realities of life, we now partake of this bread. Enable us to find faith in distress, hope in despair and love in hatred. To the immortal cross be glory time beyond time and space beyond space. Amen.

* * * *

Our Father, we thank Thee for this loaf. Wilt Thou sustain our faith as we partake of it. Enable us to gain that intelligent conviction which gives courage and hope, though we walk in the shadow of death. In our savior's name. Amen.

Lord's Table

Bread

O Lord, like a torch in the dark the cross gleams in our hearts. As we partake of this precious loaf, may it truly feed our faith. Enable us to follow the gleam of Thy cross till the cycle of life marks its end. Through Jesus Christ, our lord. Amen.

* * * * *

O God, we thank Thee for Thy providence that has brought us together to this Thy own table. As we feed upon the bread from heaven, help us to reflect upon the true significance of this ordinance. May our burning passion for the cross and glowing faith in Thy word guide us in all relationships of man. In Jesus' name we pray. Amen.

Note: "Providence" means benevolent guidance of God. "Ordinance" signifies authoritative command.

Lord's Table

Bread

In the turmoil of human experiences, we now feel the tranquility of the radiant cross. We thank Thee for that cross that has conquered chaos and put the universe in order. As we commemorate that very cross which surpasses time and space, may we learn to nourish our souls with the bread from heaven. Enable us to feed upon faith, hope and love. Through Jesus Christ, our lord. Amen.

Scripture: I Corinthians 13:13.

* * * * *

Our heavenly Father, we thank Thee for this loaf, the symbol of our lord's broken body. We stand beneath the cross. We behold Thy son, even Thy only son. Help us to lay ourselves on that cross. Enable us to enter into the fellowship of his suffering. May we share that cross with our fellowmen and women. In our savior's name. Amen.

Note: The bread is regarded as an emblem or symbol among many Christians, Disciples; but in some churches the bread is thought to be the body of the Christ.

Lord's Table

Bread

We thank Thee for Jesus, for he shattered our bonds. We thank Thee for the cross, for it made us free. We thank Thee for this bread, for it renews our covenant. May we be ever grateful for Thy saving grace. Wilt Thou set our hearts aflame with zeal for the Christ. In his name we pray. Amen.

* * * * *

O Thou, lord of light and lord of love, we thank Thee for this blessed bread from heaven. As we partake of this feast of Thy grace, may the vision of the cross rise before us. Grant us the torch of Christian light. Guard us with the shield of Christian love. Enable us at last to share the burden of the cross. In our savior's name. Amen.

Lord's Table

Bread

We thank Thee, O God, for the rustling of leaves, the song of birds, the calmness of the starlit eve, and the splendor of the sunlit dawn. With eager devotion do we partake of this bread. As Thou hast given us Thy only son, so may we learn to sacrifice ourselves for our neighbor. We dedicate ourselves to Thee, O God. Manifest Thy love through us in the turmoil of the human world, and the struggle of human life. In Jesus' name we pray. Amen.

Note: The most common Hebrew word translated "neighbor" means friend or companion. The Greek word often so rendered signifies one who is near or close.

* * * * *

We thank Thee for this loaf. Humbly do we enter the golden portals of redeemed life. May the peace of the silvery moon be our guiding light, even as we walk in the shadow of death. In Jesus' name we pray. Amen.

Note: "Shadow of death" reminds one of Psalm 23:4. Here, however, "valley of darkness" is preferred to "valley of the shadow of death."

Lord's Table

Bread

O Lord, humbly do we partake of this heavenly loaf. Wilt Thou cleanse us of our earthly transgressions, and render our souls into the beauty and purity of snow. In our savior's name. Amen.

* * * * *

Our Father in heaven, quicken our humble hearts as we partake of this heavenly loaf. Enable us to enter into the mystery of Thy saving grace. In our savior's name. Amen.

Lord's Table

Bread

We thank Thee, O Lord, for the dawn of conscience as we approach this table of Thy own appointment. Wilt Thou bless the loaf as we partake of it. Let the glorious rays of Thy unfailing love disperse the morning mist of our selfish pride. As Thou hast ordained the renewal of nature, so may we once again realize the debt we owe to the Christ. In his precious name we pray. Amen.

*   *   *   *   *

Father, we thank Thee for the memories of the past, for the holy birth, for the wonderful ministry, and for the saving sacrifice of the Christ. May the star of Bethlehem illumine our hearts, as we partake of this loaf. In Jesus' name we pray. Amen.

74

Lord's Table

Bread

We thank Thee, O God, for the dawn of human conscience that is brought forth by the light of the New Testament. Realizing the debt we owe to our savior, do we humbly partake of this holy loaf. May our Christian faith guide us till the cycle of life marks its end. Through Jesus Christ we pray. Amen.

*   *   *   *   *

O Thou, Lord of the universe and Father of mankind, as we envision the ancient cross, how can we forget Thy saving grace? We thank Thee for this bread of life. With humble hearts and contrite spirits, do we partake of this emblem. Enable us to embrace the gleam of Thy everlasting love, and let Thy kingdom come to this world, in which Thou hast placed us. In Jesus' name we pray. Amen.

Lord's Table

Wine

Father, we thank Thee for this fruit of the vine. As we partake of it, may we become worthy of the discipleship. Enable us to fulfill our Christian destiny with love and service, sharing the cross with the Christ. In his name we pray. Amen.

* * * * *

Father, we thank Thee for this fruit of the vine. Humbly do we partake of this heavenly feast. Wilt Thou awake our souls from the scarlet couch of sin, and restore our hearts to the golden throne of the cross. In Jesus' name we pray. Amen.

> *Note: Isaiah 1:18 says: '. . . though your sins are like scarlet, they shall be as white as snow. . . ." Amos 6:4 says: "Woe to those who . . . stretch themselves upon their couches. . . ."*

76

Lord's Table

Wine

We thank Thee for this emblematic cup of Thine own ordinance. Help us to realize its significance and its meaning. Enter into our hearts and beautify our souls. Cleanse us of our sins and Christianize anew our lives. Teach us, guide us, and lead us for the sake of Christ, O God, our redeemer and savior. In Jesus' name we pray. Amen.

> *Note: Many Christians, Disciples, regard the Lord's Supper as an ordinance, rather than a sacrament.*

* * * * *

Our heavenly Father, for the creativeness of man, which Thou hast bestowed upon us, we thank Thee. For our creative thinking we ask Thy guidance. For our creative being we ask Thy blessing. May our minds and bodies bear the mark of the cross. Help us to realize the significance of this cup. We ask this in Jesus' name. Amen.

Lord's Table

Wine

Our heavenly Father, we thank Thee for this fruit of the vine, the emblem of the precious blood of the Christ shed for the remission of our sins. As we partake of this cup may we truly realize the debt we owe to him who became obedient unto death, that we might have abundant life. As we draw nigh unto Thee in this sacred ordinance, enable us to walk humbly with our savior to the end that we may grow in his image. For we ask this in his name. Amen.

Note: Many Christians, Disciples, use grape juice as the emblem of the blood of the Christ. In some churches real wine has been served. For some Christian people the communion wine is thought to become the blood of Jesus.

* * * * *

In the quietude of this moment, we most humbly come to Thee, our heavenly Father. Draw us closer to Thee now and evermore by virtue of Thy mercy unto us. Show us Thy countenance, O Lord, as we partake of this cup of the New Covenant. Lead us into the gate of the eternal truth, and give us the motive for the clean and wholesome life. In our savior's name we pray. Amen.

Note: "New Covenant" signifies Christian agreement with God.

Lord's Table

Wine

Our gracious Father, we thank Thee for Thy only son, the savior of all mankind, in whose memory this feast is held. As we partake of this cup, may our souls follow in the footsteps of our lord, from the garden of Gethsemane to the cross of Calvary. Enable us to realize more fully the debt we owe to him for our redemption, and to become more conscious of the meaning of the Christian life. Use us, as Thou wilt, for the glory of him who died for us. In his name we pray. Amen.

> *Note: The phrase, "only begotten son," which appears in older English versions of the Bible, is acceptable. But "only son" conveys the same meaning.*

* * * * *

Our heavenly Father, we thank Thee for our Christian experiences and memories. In the bright sunshine, under the dark and cloudy sky, day unto day, and night unto night, the Christ is our strength and guide. As we partake of this wine, may we once again embrace his saving grace. Let it indeed sustain us now and during the rest of this week. In Jesus' name we pray. Amen.

Lord's Table

Wine

We thank Thee, our heavenly Father, for this sacred ordinance of our lord's own appointing. In the quietude of meditation, we beseech Thee, O Lord. As we partake of this fruit of the vine, the emblem of our lord's shed blood, may our souls follow him from the garden of Gethsemane to the cross of Calvary, and may we thus enter into the fellowship of his suffering. Enable us to live, move and have our being in Thee. For we ask in Jesus' name. Amen.

> *Note: "Ordinance" is an authoritative command. Many Christians, Disciples, regard the bread and the wine of the sacred communion as emblems of the body and the blood of the Christ.*

* * * * *

Lord, blessed Lord, there is none beside Thee. We thank Thee for this cup of Thy grace, reminding us of the remission of our sins, and the conquest over death. Grant us the shield of faith. Give us the sword of the spirit. Let us follow the gleam of the cross now and evermore. Amen.

Scripture: Ephesians 6:16-17.

Lord's Table

Wine

We thank Thee, our Father, for this blessed cup. With contrite spirits do we enter the golden portals of redeemed life. May the truth of the ancient cross be our strength, may the light of the beaming star be our guide, and may the peace of the silvery moon be our refuge, as we stagger under the burden of life. In Jesus' name we pray. Amen.

* * * * *

Father of mankind, we thank Thee for this feast of the New Covenant. May this fruit of the vine symbolize the redeeming blood of the Christ. May this blood of the Christ signify his conquest over death. Enslave us, we pray, with the bejeweled chains of Thy love. Enable us, we ask, to bathe in the golden sunshine of Thy light. In Jesus' name. Amen.

> *Note: The sacred communion is the feast of the New Covenant, or the feast commemorating the Christian agreement with God. This involves one's confession of faith in the Christ, and one's commitment to his cause.*

81

Lord's Table

Wine

Our Father, Father of all mankind, we thank Thee for this blessed symbol of redeemed life. As we partake of this cup, may our lord's crown of thorns become our crown of garlands, and may his burden of the cross become our burden of love. To that eternal faith be glory, forever and ever. Amen.

* * * * *

Our heavenly Father, we thank Thee for this cup. With contrite spirit do we behold the shining star of faith. May the truth of the ancient cross be our unfailing refuge, even as we stagger under the burden of life. Through Jesus Christ, our lord. Amen.

Lord's Table

Wine

Father, humbly do we partake of this blessed cup. Wilt Thou deliver us of our worldly bonds, and grant us faith in the unfailing grace and mercy of the cross. In our savior's name we pray. Amen.

* * * * *

O Lord, we thank Thee for this fruit of the vine. As we partake of it, may our souls embrace the zeal and ardor of fire. May Thy will be done. Through Jesus Christ, our lord. Amen.

> *Note: The Hebrew word translated "soul" means individuality or person, whereas the Greek word for "soul" signifies breath as a sign of life. Other connotations of "soul" in the Bible are derived from these basic concepts.*

83

Lord's Table

Wine

Father, open our spiritual eyes as we partake of this blessed cup. Help us to grow into the image of Thy beloved son. In his name we pray. Amen.

* * * * *

Like a torch in the dark, the cross gleams in our hearts. Like a fountain in the desert, Jesus quenches thirsting souls. May this fruit of the vine feed our faith. Help us to follow the gleam of the cross. Help us to drink at the fountain of life, lest we die, O Lord, lest our souls die. In our savior's name we pray. Amen.

Note: The "fountain of life" appears in such passages as Psalm 36:9; Proverb 13:14 and 14:27. "Souls" in this prayer signifies persons.

Lord's Table

Wine

O God, Thou hast brought forth the universe out of chaos and appointed man to rule over Thy creation. We praise Thy name. As we partake of this blessed cup, may we attain the mighty power of the cross. May we not be overcome by mundane disappointment and despair, but may we grow into the image of him who died for us. In his holy name we pray. Amen.

Scriptures: Genesis 1:1-2:1; Psalm 33:6-7; Isaiah 45:7-13.

Note: According to the Hebrew text Isaiah 45:8-13 is a unit, and verse 7 concludes the preceding unit of thought.

* * * *

We thank Thee, our Father, for the cross. As we partake of this cup, wilt Thou implant in our hearts the virtues of the cross. May it be our life's guide in all human associations, today, tomorrow, in the wake of birth, and in the shadow of death. In Jesus' name we pray. Amen.

Lord's Table

Wine

O Lord, God of the universe and Father of mankind, we thank Thee for the Christ, the true incarnate of Thyself and the veritable flesh of Thy word. In token of our faith in his victory over death, do we partake of this fruit of the vine. May it become a seed planted in our soul, never dying and ever growing, until we may be led by Thy grace to the perfect peace, world without end. In his name. Amen.

> *Note: "Incarnate" means that which has been made into flesh, and "veritable" true or real. "Peace" in the Bible signifies not only the cessation of war, but that which is sound or healthy, or that which is complete.*

* * * * *

O Thou, rock of the transient world, we thank Thee for this cup of Thy grace. May our faith in the ancient cross purify every dimension of our feeling and willing. May it sanctify every sphere of our thought and action. May it magnify the Christ even unto the uttermost parts of Thy creation. We ask in his name. Amen.

> *Note: "Transient" means passing quickly or temporary, and "sanctify" to make holy or purify.*

Lord's Table

Wine

Our Father, we thank Thee for this symbol of the grapes of Canaan. Awake our souls from the scarlet couch of transgressions. Restore our hearts to the golden throne of the cross. In our savior's name we pray. Amen.

Note: "Canaan" is the area commonly known as Palestine. Today it consists of the State of Israel and the portion on the west side of the Jordan which once belonged to the Hashemite Kingdom of Jordan.

* * * *

O Lord, more precious than gold is Thy son. More glorious than gems is Thy kingdom. More powerful than the sword is Thy word. We thank Thee for this fruit of the vine. Help us to conquer the whole creation with the light of the cross. In Jesus' name we pray. Amen.

Note: In one of the Dead Sea Scrolls "the children of light" war against "the children of darkness," and in this war the former are triumphant over the latter. The contrast between light and darkness, good and evil, and spirit and flesh is familiar to the student of the Bible.

Lord's Table

Wine

O Thou, creator of the universe, we thank Thee for Thy boundless love. Realizing our unworthiness, do we humbly partake of this wine. May the glory of the cross illumine burdened souls and darkened hearts, in the depth below without limit and in the height above without end. We abide in Thee, O great spirit. Abide in us forevermore. Amen.

> *Note: Wine, instead of water, was commonly drunk in Palestine, as it is today. Water is scarce, and it is not always safe to drink.*

* * * * *

O Lord, we thank Thee for the saving power of the cross of Jesus. May our conscience be reborn, may our lives be renewed, and may our homes be rebuilt upon the rock of salvation, as we partake of this wine. In our savior's name we pray. Amen.

> *Note: Drinking (of liquor) is not condemned in the Bible, but drunkenness is. However, the Aaronites were prohibited to drink when they went into the tent of meeting (Leviticus 10:8-9), and the Nazirites were not permitted to drink (Numbers 6:2-3).*

Lord's Table

Wine

O Lord, we thank Thee for the Christ, ever approachable, though never reachable. As we partake of this cup, wilt Thou draw us closer to that perfect person, even Thy only son. Once again do we dedicate ourselves to Thee. Wilt Thou strengthen our faith in the cross. In our savior's name. Amen.

* * * * *

O Lord, God of hosts and Father of mankind, we thank Thee for this heavenly feast of the New Covenant. With utmost humility do we partake of this cup of Thy salvation. Enable us to drink from the fountain of eternal life. Help us to walk in the path of Thy divine light. Grant, O Lord, that we share the precious love of our blessed lord with all mankind. Glory be to the ancient cross, now and forevermore. Amen.

Note: "New Covenant" signifies the solemn Christian agreement with God, compared to the old agreement under Mosaic authority.

Lord's Table

Wine

O Thou, merciful Father, we thank Thee for this blessed fruit of the vine. As we humbly partake of it, wilt Thou grant us courage when we are discouraged, strength when we are weak, Thy guiding light when we go astray, and Thy comforting spirit when we stagger under the burden of the cross. To that cross of Christ be glory forever and ever. Amen.

* * * * *

O Thou, gracious God and merciful Father, we thank Thee for this our faith in Thy revealed word, for this Thy table of the New Covenant, and for this sacred emblem of the risen lord. As we feed upon this fruit of the vine, may we truly partake of the nature of the Christ. Recreate us, and remold us according to Thy will, and let us live in peace for Thy sake. Through Jesus Christ, our lord. Amen.

Note: "Revealed word" here means Jesus. See John 1:14. "New Covenant" is Christian agreement with God, involving one's confession and commitment.

Lord's Table

Wine

Blessed be Thou, O Lord, whose boundless mercy brought us here to this table of the New Covenant. We thank Thee for this fruit of the vine. As we humbly partake of it, may the shining star of heaven enter our hearts, and may it illumine our pathway of life with the divine light above. Let our Christian faith and deeds blossom into the flower of eternal life. For we ask through Jesus Christ, our lord. Amen.

> *Note: "New Covenant" is the solemn new agreement with God, compared to the old agreement under Mosaic authority. The former is Christian, and the latter is Jewish, but they are closely related to each other.*

* * * *

New Year

In the quest of the ultimate truth, we submit ourselves to Thee, O God, for Thou art the author of all, the creator of all, and father of all mankind. May the threshold of this new year mark our steadfast advance towards Christian perfection. Let the bread of heaven strengthen our feet staggering under the heavy burden of the cross. In our savior's name we pray. Amen.

91

Lord's Table

New Year

Our Father in heaven, we thank Thee for Thy providence that has brought us to these precious moments of communion with Thee. May the mystic power of this ordinance transmute the darker hours of yesteryear into the brighter days of the new year, and our earthly lives of yesteryear into the consecrated souls of the new year. Henceforth, let our renewed virtues guide us, and our reawakened faith sustain us, as we press onward towards the perfect image of the Christ. In his name. Amen.

* * * * *

Palm Sunday

We thank Thee, O God, for the victorious entry of the Christ into Jerusalem, and for his ultimate conquest over death. Hosanna in the highest! May the recurring spring symbolize the cross of Calvary. May the bread of life emblematize the lamb of God. May the vision of the Last Supper rise before us as we partake of this feast. In Christ's name. Amen.

Scriptures: Matthew 21:9; 26:17-29; Mark 11:10; 14:12-25; John 1:29; I Corinthians 11:23-26; Revelation 1:29.

Note: "Hosanna" consists of two Hebrew words, hosha' meaning "Save!", and na' "please!"

Lord's Table

Easter

Praised be Thou, O Lord, for Thou hast created life, renewing itself in nature and man. We thank Thee for this renewal of the covenant with Thee. As we humbly participate in this sacred rite, may we truly sense the emergence of new life out of dying self, and may this new life blossom into the glorious beauty of everlasting spring. Let our thoughts, words and deeds embrace the purity of the Easter lily and the innocence of the risen Christ. In his name we pray· Amen.

Note: "Covenant" is an agreement and "rite" a solemn ceremony or observance.

*　*　*　*　*

Spring

O Thou, Lord of our destiny, we thank Thee for this table of Thy grace, and for this emblem of Thy love. As we partake of this manna from heaven (fruit of the vine), may we truly renew our covenant with Thee. Henceforth, let us grow day by day into the image of the Christ, and let us blossom into the beauty of Thy holiness as Thy flowers of the spring. To this end, our Father, grant us Thy divine peace, as we share the burden of the cross. Through Jesus Christ, our lord. Amen.

Note: "Manna" is the "bread from heaven." See Exodus 16:4,15,31, etc· The "divine peace" connotes much more than the cessation of war. It means completeness or perfectness.

Lord's Table

Spring

O Lord, God of eternity, creator of the universe, and Father of mankind. We praise Thy name. We thank Thee for this sacred emblem of the imperishable body (blood) of the Christ. May it truly render us anew, so that we may worthily walk in Thy light. Though the recurring beauty of the spring may perish, let us embrace the infinite beauty of Thy holiness. Though the mountains fall and seas rage, let Thy peace prevail over us, world without end. In our savior's name we pray. Amen.

Note: The expression "walk" in the Bible sometimes means to live or manner of life.

* * * * *

Blessed be Thou, O Lord, for Thy creative wisdom and redeeming love. We thank Thee for this heavenly feast of the New Covenant, and for this divine symbol of our savior. As nature begins to wear the raiment of the spring, so clothe us with the garment of renewed life. As Thou hast enshrined in nature the power of revival, so instill within us the reborn faith in Christ Jesus. Let Thy word be fulfilled. Let the ancient cross illumine our hearts, this day and forevermore. Amen.

Lord's Table

Spring

Blessed Father of all mankind, we thank Thee for the passion of Jesus Christ, whose shame and loss have released us from the bond of sin and death. May the mystery of this holy communion transmute our suffering to joy, and transform our turmoil to peace. May the beauty of the spring tide embellish our souls with faith, hope and love. In our savior's name. Amen.

* * * * *

Summer

Lord of the universe and Father of Mankind, in the quietude of this summer morn and in the silence of reverent bliss, do we look up unto Thee and praise Thy name. We thank Thee for this sacred emblem. May we truly meet Thee afresh, as we participate in this holy communion. Henceforth, let us live anew for Thy sake. So strengthen us and guide us according to Thy will, to the end that our daily thoughts, words and deeds will proclaim Thy saving grace. In Jesus' name we pray. Amen.

Note: To many Christians including the Disciples, the bread and wine are the emblems; but other Christians believe that they truly become the body and blood of the Christ at the communion.

95

Lord's Table

Autumn

We thank Thee, O precious Father, for the manifestation of Thy power of resurrection, which Thou hast enshrined in nature and man. In memory of the crown of Thy creation, even Thy own word incarnate, do we humbly partake in this sacred feast of the New Covenant. Though flowers fade and leaves fall, let us recall Thy blessing of the summer fruits. When human strength wanes and earthly wisdom fails, let us remember the Christ's victory over death. Grant us peace, now and evermore. Amen.

> *Note: "Incarnate" means made into flesh. Jesus is thought to be God's word in human form. During the summer months, it rarely rains in Palestine; but many fruits ripen then. See Jeremiah 40:10,12.*

* * * *

O Lord, our God, and Father of mankind, we thank Thee for this feast of the New Covenant and for our Lord's victory over death. May this precious emblem instill within us a renewed faith in the ancient cross. When autumnal leaves fall, help us to remember the spring to come. When the day is dark, let us visualize the sun, the moon and the stars of Thy creation. When we stagger under our burdens of life, may we realize Thy sustaining hand of love. Through Jesus Christ, our lord, we pray. Amen.

Lord's Table

Autumn

Lord of the universe and savior of mankind, we thank Thee for the autumnal brocade without, the gleaming cross within, and this emblematic table before us. With grateful hearts and contrite spirits, do we partake of this fruit of the vine, and we pray that we may regain that purity of faith in trust like unto that of a babe on its mother's bosom. May the spiritual stars of Thy tender mercy illumine our pathway of life, though the day be dark, though the burden be grave. In Jesus' name. Amen.

* * * * *

Lord of the universe, God of mankind, our Father. We thank Thee for the precious sacrifice of Jesus Christ, for this priceless table of the New Covenant, and for this life-giving emblem of Thy love. As we enter into the divine mystery of the Eucharist, let our souls die with the Christ, and let our souls rise with him. Weave us together in that harmonious beauty which manifests itself in the golden brocade of colorful autumnal leaves. Let us live for Thy sake. In our savior's name. Amen.

Note: "Eucharist" signifies thankfulness or gratitude. This is another designation of the holy communion.

Lord's Table

Autumn

Praised and exalted be Thy name, O God of the universe and Father of mankind. In the quietude of autumnal glory and in the beauty of Thy holiness, do we humbly bow before Thee, so that we may meet Thee afresh. Accept our thanksgiving, hear our supplications, and bless this table of Thine own appointment. Cleanse us, remold us, remake us, and use us according to Thy will. We rededicate ourselves to Thy cause. Have mercy upon us. Have mercy upon us. Amen.

* * * *

Winter

Our Father, in these precious moments of quietude, do we look up unto Thee and praise Thy name. We thank Thee for this commemoration of Thy saving grace in Jesus Christ. May this act of our participation cleanse us, and render us as white and pure as the snow which covers the handiwork of man this morning. Glory be to Thy own handiwork, even the Church of Christ. In our savior's name we pray. Amen.

Lord's Table

> *Winter*

We thank Thee, our heavenly Father, for this sacred loaf. As we partake of it, may our characters attain the beauty and purity of snow. May Thy kingdom come. Through Jesus Christ, our savior, we pray. Amen·

*   *   *   *   *

> *Offering*

We thank Thee, our Father, for this opportunity to return to Thee a portion of that abundance that Thou hast given us. Cleanse it, and use it as Thou wilt for the glory of him who died for us. In his name. Amen.

Offering

Father, we have dedicated ourselves to Thee. May this humble token of our devotion to Thy cause be acceptable in Thy sight. In Jesus' name. Amen.

* * * * *

As we have rededicated ourselves to Thee, our Father, so do we humbly express our gratitude in this thanksgiving. Consecrate this humble gift to the great cause for which the Christ died for us. In his name we pray. Amen.

Offering

The earth is Thine, and the fulness thereof. We are Thine, and all
that we possess. As we surrender to Thee a small portion of the
abundance that Thou hast given us, we pray that Thou wilt bless
it, purify it and use it for the glory of the Christ. In his name.
Amen.

Scriptures: Psalm 24:1; I Corinthians 10:26.

*Note: ". . . the fulness thereof" is found in the King
James Version and in the American Revised Version.
The Revised Standard Version renders thus in Psalm
24:1; but in Psalm 50:12 this version has ". . . all that is in
it" for exactly the same Hebrew expression, and in I
Corinthians 10:26 ". . . everything in it" which is an in-
direct translation of the Greek text.*

* * * * *

As the Christ gave up himself that we may have eternal life, so
do we humbly express our faith in this thank-offering. May it be
acceptable unto Thee, O merciful God. For we ask in Jesus' name.
Amen.

Offering

We thank Thee for Thy beloved son. Wilt Thou bless this portion of our rededication to him. To him be glory forever and ever. In his name. Amen.

* * * * *

Father, we thank Thee for Thy saving grace and for Thy beloved son· Wilt Thou bless this humble portion of our rededication to his cause. Glory be unto Thee now and forevermore. Amen.

Offering

We thank Thee, our heavenly Father, for this opportunity to glorify the Christ. Not that Thou seekest for our gifts, but that we may receive the spiritual benefit for Christ's sake, we bring these offerings unto Thee. Cleanse them and use them according to Thy will. In our savior's name we pray. Amen.

* * * * *

Offering

Winter

O Lord, may this small offering become a ray of the sunshine, and a drop of showers which usher in the Christian spring to this wintry and unbelieving world. In Christ's name we pray. Amen.

Benediction

Bible

The Lord bless thee, and keep thee: The Lord make his face to shine upon thee, and be gracious unto thee: The Lord lift up his countenance upon thee, and give thee peace. Amen.

Scripture: Numbers 6:24-26.

Note: This is called priestly benediction. One should be free to use "you" for "thee" and "to" for "unto," as does the Revised Standard Version.

* * * * *

The grace of the Lord Jesus Christ, and the love of God, and the communion of the Holy Ghost, be with you all. Amen.

Scripture: II Corinthians 13:14.

Note: This is called apostolic benediction. One may use "fellowship" for "communion" and "Holy Spirit" for "Holy Ghost" as do many recent English translations.

Bible

Let the words of my mouth, and the meditation of my heart, be acceptable in thy sight, O Lord, my strength, and my redeemer. Amen.

Scripture: Psalm 19:14.

Note: Here perhaps "my rock" is preferable to "my strength."

* * * * *

God be merciful unto us, and bless us; and cause his face to shine upon us; that thy way may be known upon earth, thy saving health among all nations. Amen.

Scripture: Psalm 67:1-2.

Note: Here one may say "thy salvation" instead of "thy saving health."

Benediction

Bible

Now unto him that is able to do exceeding abundantly above all that we ask or think, according to the power that worketh in us, unto Him be glory in the church by Christ Jesus throughout all ages, world without end. Amen.

Scripture: Ephesians 3:20-21.

Note: "... and in Christ Jesus...." is perhaps better than "... by Christ Jesus." Familiar quotations are given here and elsewhere, even if they are not good translations.

* * * * *

The peace of God, which passeth all understanding, shall keep your hearts and minds in Christ Jesus. Amen.

Scripture: Philippians 4:7.

Benediction

Bible

Now unto the King eternal, immortal, invisible, the only God, be honor and glory for ever and ever. Amen.

Scripture: I Timothy 1:17.

Note: ". . . the King eternal" may be rightly rendered ". . . the king of ages," as in the Revised Standard Version, or ". . . the King of all worlds," as in the New English Bible.

* * * * *

Now unto him that is able to guard you from stumbling, and to set you before the presence of his glory without blemish in exceeding joy, to the only God our Savior, through Jesus Christ our Lord, be glory, majesty, dominion and power, before all time, and now, and for evermore. Amen.

Scripture: Jude 24-25.

Note: The word "authority" instead of "power" may be used. The former is a proper translation of the Greek word, and is found in the Revised Standard Version.

Benediction

O Thou, guardian of our souls, teach us, guide us in our humble ministry, and may glory be to the ancient cross this day, and forevermore! Amen.

> *Note: Ministry signifies service. It may not be limited to the function of professional ministers. Each Christian should be a minister of God, and of fellow men and women.*

* * * * *

O Master, we are thine. Enable us to abide in that steadfast peace, which surpasses human understanding and which Thou alone canst give. Through Jesus Christ we pray. Amen.

> *Note: Biblical concept of peace is far more than Greek or Latin or English may imply. Its primary meaning is completeness. Hence, healthiness or perfection. The Hebrew word for it is shalom, which is a very common greeting in modern Hebrew. Islam is derived from the same Semitic origin.*

Benediction

May the lamp of Thy perfect wisdom illumine our minds, guard our course, and guide us to the higher destiny of Thy peace. Through Jesus Christ· Amen.

* * * * *

May God, the giver of peace, who brought back from the dead our lord Jesus, the great shepherd of the sheep, fit you by every blessing to do his will, and through him carry out in you what will please him. To him be glory forever and ever. Amen.

SCHOOL

Chapel

Father of steadfast love, accept our thanks as we bow before Thee at the beginning of this hour of meditation for all that which is good in our lives. Help us to realize that Thy constant care has brought us again to this period of prayer. May it be with rejoicing hearts that we approach Thee in prayer. Forgive our sins, and help us not to do what is unnecessary, but to do what is important in Thy sight. May we examine ourselves once more in the light of Jesus' teachings, and strive towards the higher goals of life. May we thus become better disciples of the Christ at the end of this service. In his name we pray. Amen.

Note: "Steadfast love" is a more recent translation of the Hebrew word which was formerly rendered "loving-kindness" or "mercy." There are, of course, several other English words applicable for it such as "kindness," "love" and "pious affection." For the repetitive usage of this word, see Psalm 136.

Chapel

O God, who art the source of universal intelligence and cosmic energy, we praise Thy name. We thank Thee for the ordered knowledge of higher learning. May that knowledge, motivated by Thy will, manifest itself in all human relationships in such a way as may be acceptable in Thy sight. We now invoke Thy blessings upon this service. May we grasp its significance for Thy own sake and for the sake of human betterment. In our savior's name we pray· Amen.

Note: "knowledge" in the Bible has much to do with the knowledge of God based upon experience such as meeting Him and talking with Him, rather than the ordered knowledge of man. This human knowledge should be controlled by God's will.

Commencement

Magnified and sanctified be Thy name, O God, our heavenly Father. We praise Thy name, for with abundant mercy Thou hast nurtured us, and with tender care Thou hast brought us to this day of commencement. May Thy guiding spirit rest upon this assembly, and may this become truly the day of our commencing wholehearted rededication to Thy cause. As we stand in Thy presence, enable us to realize that every moment and every place afford us the opportunity for Thy ministry, and every man and every woman present the need for Thy saving grace. And now may Thy divine spirit rekindle our flickering torch in the dark, and let it blaze its way to illumine every corner of Thy creation, to the end that all mankind may walk humbly in Thy light. To Jesus, the Christ, be glory forever and ever. Amen·

* * * * *

Honor Day

O Lord, how excellent is Thy name. From the temple-schools of Babylonia to the court academies of Egypt, and from the forest colleges of India to the urban universities of America, the pearls of wisdom adorn the golden string of progress. But, O Lord, may it be from Zion that Thy wisdom whispers to our conscience. Let us bathe our intellect in the grace of Thy intellect. May Thy blessings rest upon this gathering and this institution of learning, as we honor the scholastic crown of glory, for we ask in our savior's name. Amen.

Blessed be Thou, O Lord, Lord of wisdom, wisdom of the east, wisdom of the west, wisdom of the past, and wisdom of the present. We praise Thy name. Grant us, we pray, the guiding star of principle which may order human knowledge in harmony with Thy will. Through Jesus Christ, our lord. Amen.

Note: "Wisdom" in the Bible is that skill which translates thought into action according to God's will. In the New Testament the Christ is identified with the wisdom of God. See I Corinthians 1:24,30; Colossians 2:2-3, etc. "Knowledge" is that understanding which is based on experience, in many passages of the Bible.

Founders' Day

Blessed be Thou, O Lord, for the crown of Thy glory, for the
scepter of Thy wisdom, and for the armor of our faith. We thank
Thee for Thy gracious providence that has guided the growth of
this institution of learning, for the prophetic vision of its founders,
and for the words and deeds of its distinguished graduates. May
Thy continued blessings rest upon the constituent divisions, colleges and schools; and may the woof of knowledge and skill now
available in these academic halls and the warp of the ideas and
ideals of the founders create an unending golden brocade for
tomorrow. Bless this gathering to this end, and to this end we
pray. In our savior's name. Amen.

> *Note: A university usually consists of colleges and
> schools. Generally speaking, colleges have undergraduate
> students, whereas schools have graduate students, in the
> United States of America. Divisions are sometimes sec-
> tions of curricula, and other times parts of the entire
> university organization.*

O Lord, we thank Thee for the Christian memories and experiences that have been ours during the past year. We thank Thee, above all, for the intellectual gift that has been bestowed upon us; but wilt Thou forbid that we become too proud of it to be truly Christian. Help us to attain intelligent faith, hope and love; but prohibit that we become too arrogant to become really Christlike. May we forevermore walk humbly with him who died for us. In his name. Amen.

Note: Written for the annual banquet of a Christian college.

Praised, exalted and extolled be Thy name, O God, creator of the universe and Father of mankind. We thank Thee for Thy providence that has nurtured this nation with Thy guiding spirit and tender care, for the heroes and heroines of the past who upheld the integrity of this government, and for the men and women of today and tomorrow who devote their lives to the safety of this Republic and to the peace of the world. And now, O God, we invoke Thy blessing upon these cadets who are about to be commissioned here. Wilt Thou watch over them as they assume the duties and responsibilities placed in their hands, and may they in some measure enhance the ideals represented by the stars and stripes of our flag. To this end we pray. Amen.

Note: Some cadets were Jewish. Hence, the lack of Jesus Christ in this prayer. In any meeting of the Church, however, there shall be no hesitancy in calling upon Jesus, regardless of the contents of the audience.

Installation of Faculty

    Seminary

O Lord, the glory of ancient Babylonia sleeps in the mounds of the Euphrates. The splendor of ancient Egypt rests in the ruins of the Nile. But it was the voice crying in the wilderness of Judea that heralded the majesty of Thy living word· May this faculty magnify the cross. May this institution exalt Thy kingdom. To the Christ, our king, be glory forever and ever. Amen.

    Scriptures: Isaiah 40:3-5; Luke 3:4-6; John 1:1-5.

✻   ✻   ✻   ✻   ✻

Thanksgiving

    America

O Thou, God of our fathers, and Father of all mankind. We thank Thee for Thy providence that has placed us upon this galaxy of all galaxies, upon this planet of all planets, and in this nation of all nations on earth. We thank Thee for this beautiful America, with its purple mountains and amber waves of grain, with its spacious skies above and fertile soil below, and with liberty in life and justice in law. We thank Thee for our heroes of the past and heroines of yore, who founded this nation and nurtured its destiny, until now when fifty stars shine in one accord in our flag. As heirs of this precious heritage, we humbly pray for that wisdom and that faith which may enhance Thy name from glory to glory, world without end. Amen.

Christmas

Praised be Thou, O Lord, creator of the universe and Father of mankind. We thank Thee for the order which Thou hast ordained in nature, for the intelligence with which Thou hast endowed mankind, and for that word which Thou hast granted to the world. May the significance of that which is true, that which is good, and that which is beautiful prevail in our academic pursuits, and may we indeed become the bearers of the shining torch of brotherly love and eternal peace. To this end bless this gathering according to Thy will, for we ask in our savior's name. Amen.

Note: The "word which Thou hast granted to the world" is none other than Jesus, who is the incarnate word of God. See John 1:14. "Christmas" is not found in the Bible. Not all Christians observe Christmas on December 25th, and some Christians do not celebrate it at all.

* * * * *

Easter

Praised be Thou, O Lord, for Thy creative wisdom that Thou hast enshrined in the universe. We thank Thee for the circuit of heavenly luminaries and the cycle of earthly seasons, which brought forth once again the song of birds and the smile of flowers. We pray that the academic urge of youth clad in the scholastic raiment of the spring grow into that maturity of ideas, ideals and skills, which may be acceptable in Thy sight. May Thy intellect nurture our souls to the end that at last we may embrace the perfect image of the Christ. In his name we pray. Amen.

Note: There is no Easter mentioned in the Bible, except in Acts 12:4, according to the King James Version. It should be Passover instead, as in other versions.

119

Benediction

Mighty God, merciful Father, may the galaxy of stars of wisdom abide in Thy peace, and perpetuate the generations of man. For Thy peace we hope. For Thy peace we wait. For Thy peace we pray. Amen.

> *Note: God's peace includes much more than the cessation of war. It signifies rather the perfection of man by virtue of the divine grace. It is a result of man's wholehearted devotion to God.*

* * * * *

O Thou, Lord of light and intelligence, enable us to shatter the bonds of ignorance and egotism, and let the shining torch of knowledge bring forth the surge of our zeal for the Christ. To his cross be glory, forever and ever. Amen.

Benediction

May it be Thy will that mankind will embrace Thy wisdom and Thy peace. For this grace we pray. Amen.

> *Note: God's wisdom far surpasses the wisdom of man, and His peace excels man-made peace. God's wisdom enables man to live according to His will; and His peace endows him with saintliness.*

* * * * *

O Thou, Lord of light and wisdom, let the morning star of Thy intelligence guide the leaders of mankind. Let the evening star of Thy peace abide in the hearts of men. Let the sun and the moon of Thy order prevail throughout the world. Amen.

> *Note: God's intelligence enables one to discern how to live according to His will; and God's peace grants one perfect satisfaction in life.*

MISCELLANEA

General

May Thy name be praised. May Thy church be exalted. May the Christ be glorified. Hear our prayers, O Lord. Amen·

Note: "Name" in this prayer signifies the person. It is the same as God himself. Today in modern Hebrew "The Name" means God.

* * * *

We thank Thee, O God, for the lamp of Thy word, for the light of Thy law, and for Thy path of eternal life. Guide us and lead us in that path of Christ, now and evermore. Amen.

Note: The Hebrew word translated "law" in our English Bible means teaching or direction·

O Thou, rock of the transient world, we thank Thee for the light of Thy word and the testimonies of the pious. Have mercy upon us, lest we should lose our footing. Let Thy countenance shine upon us, lest we should succumb to temptation. Teach us Thy statutes. Grant us good judgment. Guide us in the path of grace. Lead us at last to the fountain of living water. Amen.

Scripture: Psalm 119:129-136.

Note: "Rock" is used for God in several passages of the Bible such as Psalm 18:2, and Pslam 31:3. "Transient" means passing quickly or fleeting.

* * * * *

We humbly approach Thee, O God, trusting in Thy mercy unto us. Help us to realize the limitations in human understanding, and so to maintain our faith at all times. May we not be troubled with the success of the unrighteous, but may we believe in Thy design of the universe. Enable us to cultivate our Christian courage, wisdom and insight, and thus to follow in the footsteps of our master. In his name we pray. Amen.

Scripture: Job 12:2-12.

General

Our heavenly Father, Thou are mighty and merciful. With a profound sense of humility because of our own unworthiness, we approach Thee. Wilt Thou show us Thy merciful countenance. Help us to be good members of society and faithful citizens of Thy kingdom. May we be prudent and listen to counsel. Enable us to be obedient to Thy word. Let the world understand Thee better through us, for we are Thine, forever and ever.

Scripture: Proverb 19:11-21.

* * * * *

Eternal Father, we praise Thy name, for Thou hast brought the universe from chaos into order, and from darkness unto light. Thou hast brought man from ignorance into intelligence, and from servitude unto lordship. Help us to realize the mighty power of the cross. Enable us to appreciate the supreme sacrifice of Jesus. Implant in our hearts the law of faith. In our savior's name. Amen.

Awaken our souls, O God, as we meditate upon these words. Jesus was and is the Messiah from the beginning to the end. Enable us to realize the limitations of human understanding, but help us to believe in the extent of Thy authority. Vitalize ourselves with faith to be living witnesses in Thy kingdom. May we bear and share the cross even unto the uttermost parts of the world. In our savior's name. Amen.

Scripture: Acts 1:1-11.

Note: "Messiah" means one who has been anointed. Some kings, high priests and other leaders were messiahs. However, to those who believe in Jesus, he is the Messiah. Christos, from which English Christ is derived, is the Greek translation of Hebrew messiah.

* * * * *

O Thou, the light of the world, we praise Thy name. O Thou, the rock of salvation, we adore Thy name. O Thou, the father of mankind, we glorify Thy name. Implant in our hearts the faith triumphant. Instill in our hearts the intelligence acute. In our savior's name we pray. Amen.

General

O Lord, Father of mankind, thou hast showed us the way of life through Jesus Christ. Implant in our hearts the Christian zeal for truth, honor, justice, purity, love and grace. In Jesus' name we pray. Amen.

* * * * *

O God, the glow of the cross pierces through the darkness of human turmoil Thou art our refuge. We trust Thee. Thou art our redeemer. We praise Thee. Thou art our shield. We fear not. Help us to speak Thy justice and righteousness. Enable us to gain Thy understanding and wisdom. May we abide in Thy law. In our master's name we pray. Amen.

Scripture: Psalm 37:30-40.

Note: "Justice" is the revealed will of God, and "righteousness" is that will practiced in life. "Law" signifies essentially God's teaching or directive.

General

O Lord, we come to Thee once again to reflect upon the essentials of life; and thank Thee for Thy simple gospel and the simple book. Help us to know the significance of Christian faith and experience in relation to the development of human society. May we not be haughty but may we be humble in all relationships of man. Let us become truly the disciples of the Christ. In his name we pray. Amen.

Scripture: Proverb 16:16-22.

Note: "Gospel" means good news. The act of God in the advent of the Christ is so marvelous and so profound that no human pen can fully describe it; but it is so simple that any grown-up person can appreciate it. The gospel is much easier to understand but far more difficult to practice than any philosophy or science.

America

O God, in the crimson sky of the dawn, and in the violet heaven of the eve, we humbly acknowledge the wonder of Thy handiwork. Thou hast indeed created the universe. There is none beside Thee. We thank Thee for America—beautiful not only in appearance but also in essence. May our love for Thee and for our neighbor dispel the human imperfections from this land, and magnify Thy love throughout the world. May the stars and stripes of our flag abide in Thee, now and forevermore. Amen.

Note: God is the creator of the universe according to the Bible. The most difficult creation is that of order out of chaos, and the crown of God's creation is that of saint out of sinner.

* * * * *

Bible

O Lord, author of all, all-knowing, almighty and ever-present, we praise Thy name. We thank Thee for the book of all books, even the Bible, which Thou hast freely given to all mankind. Let it not remain a sealed book which the learned ignore and the unlearned shun, but let it ever be an open book to all seekers of the truth. May the heavenly wisdom of this book dispel the eloquent wisdom of man, and restore our faith to the ancient cross of Jesus. In his name we pray. Amen.

Scriptures: Isaiah 29:9-14; I Corinthians 1:19.

Christian Growth

In the quietude of Thy glorious presence, we most humbly bow before Thee trusting in Thy mercy unto us. As learners of Thy holy word, we seek for Thy guidance in our pursuit of a better knowledge of Thy creation. As disciples of Thy only son, we seek for Thy benediction in our efforts in attaining true Christian character. As believers in Jesus, we seek for Thy blessings in our prayer for more profound and firmer faith. Wilt Thou grant us intelligence, character, and faith according to Thy will, for we are Thine to serve the Christ. In his precious name. Amen.

* * * * *

Christmas

O Lord, the voice of one that cried in the wilderness still resounds in our hearts. We thank Thee for the revelation of Thy will in Christ Jesus, Thy beloved son and exalted minister. We thank Thee for his love, so tender and so merciful that it shields even a bruised reed. We thank Thee for his word, so true and so righteous that it enlightens even a confused world. Help us to embrace a renewed faith in him, the faith which withstands even quaking earth and surging sea. In his name we pray. Amen.

Scriptures: Isaiah 40:3-5; 42:1-4; Luke 2:25-33; 3:3-6.

Cross

Divine Father.
For the cross of Jesus, we thank Thee.
Through the cross of Jesus, we approach Thee.
On the cross of Jesus, we rededicate ourselves to Thee.
Enable us to bear that cross through joys and sufferings.
To the lamb of God be glory forever and ever. Amen.

> *Note: In several passages of the New Testament, Jesus is identified with the "lamb of God." See, for example, John 1:29 and Revelation 21:14,22-23. The Greek word for "lamb" in John and that in Revelation are not the same, but either may be so rendered. However, the "lambs" in John 21:15 is the translation of the Greek word found in Revelation.*

* * * * *

Heavenly Father, let us flee for these few moments from the troubled world, so that we may again embrace the vision of the cross. We seek not the way of escape, but we do seek that faith and that courage with which to face the tasks and duties before us. Let us abide in Thee, O Lord. Abide in us if it be Thy will. In our savior's name. Amen.

131

Faith

O God, majestic, mighty and merciful. Humble words of man fail to describe Thee, but righteous hearts long for Thee. We drift in the turbulent current of this transient world. Help us, O God, to find the everlasting rock. Thou art the rock! By faith may we rest in Thy promise. By faith may we abide with Thy son. For we ask this in his name. Amen.

> *Note: God is sometimes called "my rock, and my fortress. . . ." See Psalms 18:2; 31:3; 71:3, etc. In the Hebrew language the root for the word "faith" and that for "Amen" are the same. Its derivatives are also translated "believe" and "be established" in Isaiah 7:9.*

*   *   *   *   *

O God, we thank Thee for the heroes of the past, who by virtue of their faith saw the unseen, heard the inaudible, and experienced the supernatural. Enable us to embrace that faith which perceives the ultimate cause of that which we see, hear and sense. Help us to carry on by faith the Christian ideals and Christian tasks. Strengthen our conviction that in Christ Thy promise was fulfilled. By this faith may we resurrect into eternal life. This we pray in Jesus' name. Amen.

> *Note: "Faith" in the Old Testament means essentially reliability or steadfastness, and "faith" in the New Testament belief or confidence; but both signify man's right relation to God. See Isaiah 7:9 (where "believe" and "be established" are derived from the root for "faith"); Habakkuk 2:4; Romans 4:5-22; Galatians 3:2-26; Hebrews 11:1-40.*

Faith

O Lord, from eternity unto eternity Thou art God. We thank Thee with confidence for the victory of our lord on the cross, and for Thy promise that those who believe may share in that glory. But we acknowledge our own human frailty and weakness, and pray that Thou mayest grant us that victorious faith in despair, distress and disappointment. Through Jesus Christ, our lord. Amen.

Scriptures: Isaiah 25:8; I Corinthians 15:54-57; Hebrews 12:1-2; I John 5:4.

* * * * *

Freedom

Our heavenly Father, as Thou hast given freedom to the enslaved Israel, so hast Thou graciously set us free. As Thou hast effected release to the captive Israel, so hast Thou mercifully liberated us. As Thou hast rebuilt the ruined city of David, so hast Thou tenderly reconstructed our minds and our bodies. As we praise Thy name for all these, may we evermore realize our Christian duties and responsibilities as free men and women in Christ. Use us, we pray, Thy servants and handmaids, according to Thy will for the glory of him who died for us. In his name. Amen.

Scriptures: Exodus 13:3; Deuteronomy 5:6; Ezra 1:5-6; Jeremiah 30:18-22; John 8:32, 36; I Corinthians 7:21, 24.

Humility

Eternal God, love unexcelled, justice unsurpassed, and righteousness unequalled are Thine. Thou art indeed the Father of the Christ. May our pride in human wisdom, may the arrogance of human might, and may the complacency in human wealth vanish before Thee. Dispel vanity before us, and show us the light of the world. Grant us at last that exalted mission to preach Thy word. In Jesus' name. Amen.

Scriptures: Jeremiah 9:23-24; I Corinthians 9:15-18.

* * * * *

Our Father in heaven, we thank Thee for these few moments of meditation. Help us to examine ourselves anew. Forbid that we justify ourselves rather than Thee. Prohibit that we criticize others rather than ourselves. May we learn to respect anew those who have paved the Christian way of life for us. To Jesus who justified Thy love, who bore the cross, and who died for us, be glory forever and ever. In his name we pray. Amen.

Scripture: Job 32:1-22.

Blessed be Thy name, O Lord, for the order of Thy creation that brought forth the nourishment before us. We thank Thee for the crown of Thy creation, even the creation of the children of man, to be partakers of Thy creative intellect. May the dream of the sages of the past become a reality in this assembly· May there be neither east nor west, neither north nor south, when strong men and women thus gather together. May Thy word lighten and brighten our path towards the realization of the unity of mankind, despite the diversity of cultures. Glory be to Thy golden throne, forever and ever. Amen.

> *Note: Those who quote "Oh, East is East, and West is West, and never the Twain shall meet...." from Rudyard Kipling's "Ballad of East and West," seldom recognize its latter half, which says: "But there is neither East nor West, Border, nor Breed, nor Birth, when two strong men stand face to face, though they come from the ends of the earth."*

Knowledge

O Lord, the heavens declare Thy glory, and the firmament showeth Thy handiwork. With shame we submit ourselves to Thee for fresh consecration, because, in spite of Thy merciful command, we have not actualized our duties to the full. Though not in a literal sense (see Isaiah 5:11-12), wine and harp blind nominal Christian men and women. Wilt Thou dispel the cloud of our superficial customs and manners, and enable us to gain insight of the true knowledge of Thee. Through Jesus Christ, our Lord. Amen.

Scriptures: Psalm 19:1-4; Isaiah 5:11-17.

Note: "Knowledge" in Isaiah 5:13 means the knowledge of God, and knowledge in the Bible basically signifies that which has been acquired through experience. To know God means to become intimately familiar with Him.

* * * * *

O Thou, Lord of light and intelligence, enable us to shatter the bonds of ignorance and egotism. Grant us the shining torch of knowledge which may lead us to the renewed zeal for the Christ. To his cross be glory forever and ever. Amen.

Note: "Knowledge" in this prayer is the knowledge of God, acquired through experience with Him.

Man

Lord, blessed be Thy name. As we reflect upon the glory of Thy intelligence and power, we are but the particle of dust. Yet each particle Thou hast created, and each particle is a significant element of Thy universe. Thou hast made us of this particle, but ordained us only a little lower than Thee. Thou hast bestowed on us the crown of honor, and granted us the dominion over Thy creation. We praise Thy name. Help us to attain and realize man's mission in this belwildered world. In Jesus' name we pray. Amen.

Scriptures: Genesis 1:26-28; 2:7; Psalm 8:5-8.

Note: The "angels" in Psalm 8:5 in the King James Version is derived from the Greek and Latin translations of the Hebrew word, which may be rendered "God" or "gods." Angels are occasionally referred to as "gods" in Hebrew, even though there is a definite word for them.

* * * *

Mission

O Thou, Author of all, enable us to grasp the pivot of the cross, as the line of expanding human knowledge crosses the contracting line of the universe. Dwell within us as we bear the cross. May it purify every dimension of human thought and action. May it sanctify every sphere of human feeling and willing. Yea, may it glorify even the Christ unto the uttermost parts of Thy creation. In Jesus' name we pray. Amen.

Peace

Praised be Thou, O Lord, for Thou hast given us the perfect gift of salvation. As we reflect upon our own anxiety and distress, we come to realize that we are weak within and we are imperfect without. Help us to communicate with Thee now and evermore, for Thou art our shield, our rock and our refuge. Enable us to attain that peace which, transcending every human understanding, watches over us in Christ Jesus. In his name. Amen.

Scripture: Philippians 4:4-7.

Note: Peace is a significant doctrine in Judaism and Christianity, as in some other great religions. However, the peace in the Bible has the sense of completeness or perfection. When man's relation to God is perfect, there is peace; and this is the peace that only God can give.

* * * * *

Prayer

O Lord, I am undone. I do not know how to pray, for I cannot conceive of the inner cry of each who has assembled here. But Thou knowest all. Hear us now, and enable us to hear Thy voice. In Jesus' name we pray. Amen.

Note: When one is asked to pray for others, one is often reminded of the response of Isaiah: "Woe is me! I am undone!" (Isaiah 6:5.) Yet God knows the prayer of each person. Accordingly it suffices to ask Him to hear others' prayers, if it be His will.

Prayer

We thank Thee, O Lord, for these golden moments of Christian life, when we communicate with Thee. We now behold Thy glorious countenance. We now feel Thy unfailing love. We now live, and move, and have our being in Thee. Facing the grim facts and dark realities of life, we now meditate upon Thy word. Thou art indeed our rock, our refuge, and our redeemer, O Lord. To the immortal cross be glory time beyond time, space beyond space. Amen.

Scripture: Acts 17:28.

Note: It is entirely appropriate to say "in him we exist" instead of "In him . . . have our being" in Acts 17:28. See The New English Bible. James Moffatt rendered it more than forty years ago ". . . it is in him that we . . . exist."

* * * * *

Our Father, we do not know how to pray. Yet our inner souls cry unto Thee. Enable us to offer the kind of prayer that may sustain our sense of righteousness, the kind of prayer that may glorify Thee throughout the world, and the kind of prayer that may help us to abide in Thee at peace. We pray for truly Christian prayer, O God, through Jesus Christ, our lord. Amen.

Note: Basically man can only pray that God's will be done. Man cannot believe that his will shall be done by prayer, unless it is God's will. If man's prayer controls God, that prayer leaves the realm of religion and enters the sphere of magic.

Prayer

Our Father, dispel the veil of blindness of our own egotism, and let us behold Thy countenance. Disperse the clouds of deafness of our own conceit, and let us hear Thy voice. May Thy mercy sustain us as we endeavor to live according to Thy precepts. In our savior's name. Amen.

* * * * *

Race Relations

We thank Thee, our Father, for Thy holy word that has become flesh in Jesus the Christ. We thank Thee especially for the simple fact that there is neither color line nor national boundary in Thy kingdom. Enable us to supplant disbelief with faith, despair with hope, and hatred with love. May Christian grace, trust, appreciation and goodwill be manifest in all social relationships throughout Thy creation. In our savior's name. Amen.

Scriptures: Malachi 2:10; Colossians 3:11.

Rededication

Glory be unto Thee, O Lord of the universe, and Father of mankind, for Thou hast sent us the savior of mankind. As we rededicate ourselves to his cause, let Thy wisdom dispel the pride of human wisdom, let Thy might replace the vanity of human might, and let Thy riches supplant the boast of human wealth. May the ancient cross glow in our hearts from this moment on, even like a torch in the dark. Blessed be Thou, O Lord. Blessed be Thou, O Lord. Amen.

Scripture: Jeremiah 9:23-24.

* * * * *

O God of Israel, God of the universe, and God of all mankind, great and merciful art Thou. Marvelous and wondrous are Thy gifts unto us. We thank Thee for Thy love that has been made real to us through the life of Jesus. May we live lives that are good, lives that are pure, and lives like the one of Jesus. Help us to examine ourselves and confess with shame that our lives have been far from the one exemplified by Jesus. May we consecrate ourselves anew and more fully, and give ourselves with wholehearted surrender to the task of upbuilding Thy kingdom. In our savior's name we pray. Amen.

Note: "Consecrate" means to make sacred, or set apart as holy.

Rededication

O Thou, God of steadfast love, wilt Thou accept our thanks as we bow before Thee for the reality of Thy grace unto us. Give us the sense to trace that which is true, good and beautiful in our lives unto Thee. Help us to examine ourselves before we judge others, and may we be generous with the faults of others and be kind to them. Let us be warned against failing to grow into the image of the Christ, and let us become more like him day by day. May we thus embrace Christian attitude, and practice Christian principles in our social and religious lives. Glory be unto Thee and unto Thy son. We ask in his name. Amen.

* * * * *

O God, the only God, the eternal God, there is none beside Thee. Cleanse us of our transgressions, so that we may realize inward truth. Purify us of our iniquities, so that we may embrace clean hearts. Vitalize our faith and zeal for the cross, so that with renewed spirit we may restore the joy of Thy salvation. In Jesus' name we pray. Amen.

Scripture: Psalm 51:6-14.

Rededication

We thank Thee, O God, for the burden Thou hast placed upon us. We looked for peace, but no good came, for we were not worthy of Thy cross. Help us to realize that our ultimate peace is the Christ. May the heavenly star of faith, hope and love dispel the earthly chaos of distress, despair and hate. Wilt Thou accept our humble sacrifice, as we rededicate ourselves to Thee in one body through the blood of Thy son, in whose name we pray. Amen.

Scriptures: Jeremiah 8:15, 18; Ephesians 2:11-16.

* * * * *

O God, motivate in our hearts the urge for true worship. We thank Thee for Thy church, the body of Thy only son. Enable us to become more worthy of Thy call in his service. Instill within us the riches of this mystery, the Christ. May we find joy even in the ministry of suffering. For Christ's sake. Amen.

Scripture: Colossians 1:24-29.

Rededication

Our good Father, open our spiritual eyes as we bow before Thee once again in prayer, and let us behold the splendor of Thy countenance. We thank Thee for this supreme privilege of ours to communicate with Thee, and we pray that our faults in the past for having neglected to talk with Thee may be pardoned. We thank Thee for the expansion of Thy kingdom and for the reality of Jesus. Help us to realize our responsibilities and duties as Christian men and women, and may we dedicate ourselves anew and more fully to the spread of the gospel of the Christ. In his name. Amen.

*　*　*　*　*

Amidst earthly turmoil and mundane chaos, Thy law sustaineth itself, fulfilled and graced by the Christ. We thank Thee for him, and we now commit ourselves to Thee, O God. Enable us to trust in him more earnestly. Help us to rejoice in him more faithfully. May we rest in him more peacefully. To Thee, the author of the supreme mind, be glory forever and ever. Amen.

Scripture: Psalm 37:1-7.

Note: "Mundane" means worldly, and "law" signifies teaching.

Rededication

O Thou, Master of justice, righteousness and steadfast love, we yield ourselves to Thee. Remold us, refashion us, recreate us, according to Thy will. May this prayerful response to the challenge of Thy word be acceptable in Thy sight. Make us partakers of the burden of the cross. O Lord, our shield, our rock and our redeemer. Amen.

* * * * *

O Lord, our Lord, our wills are ours to make them thine. Help us to make them so. Help us to make them Thine. Amen·

Rededication

O God, we thank Thee for the precious words of the wise. Wilt Thou remove the veil that covers the truth before us. Instill within us a spiritual balance for our words. Implant within us a qualitative scale for our expressions. Help us to know the vanity of many books. Enable us to break through the clouds of human superficialities, and let the beam of Thy divine love shine over Thy whole creation. For Jesus' sake, and in his name we pray. Amen.

Scripture: Ecclesiastes 12:9-12.

Note: Usually Ecclesiastes is considered to be a book of pessimism. However, it speaks of the truth which we ourselves experience, and some positive instructions are not lacking. See, for example, 12:1, 13.

* * * *

Almighty God, from whom flows lovingkindness to the sons of man, we praise Thy name. We marvel at Thy creation. True are Thy words. We come to Thee once again to meditate upon them. Steadfast is Thy work. We come to Thee once again to ponder over it. Enable us to realize our weakness, nay, the weakness of all human power and intelligence, and to comprehend more fully the blessed New Covenant in Jesus' blood. Thy counsel stands from eternity to eternity. And now we rededicate ourselves to Thee. May we bear the cross, world without end. In our savior's name we pray. Amen.

Scripture: Psalm 33.

Note: "Lovingkindness" or "steadfast love" appears in Psalm 33:5. It is rendered "goodness" in the King James Version. However, the Hebrew word means much more than any of these words. It has the sense of merciful and saintly piety. "New Covenant" is the Christian agreement with God, compared to the Jewish agreement.

Rededication

O God, Thy holiness transcends human emotion. Thy cross transcends human will. Thy son transcends human thought. We thank Thee for what we feel, for what we do, and for what we cogitate. We surrender to Thee, O God, our soul, our flesh, yea, our all. May unsurpassed glory crown the Christ, our king and our redeemer. In his name. Amen.

* * * * *

Sovereign

Blessed art Thou, O Lord, King of the universe, who at Thy word bringest the twilight of the eve and the dawn of the day, and who with Thy wisdom openest the gates of the heavens and the portals of faith, Thou art indeed the creater of the universe and the orderer of man's intelligence. We praise Thy name. Mayest Thou reign over us and over all mankind, for we ask in Jesus' name. Amen.

State Legislature

Blessed be Thou, O Lord, creator of the universe and father of mankind. We thank Thee for our precious America, for our beloved state, and for its officers chosen by the people of this sovereign state. Grant that Thy law abide in these lawmakers. May Thy wisdom nurture their wisdom. Let the lamp of Thy word brighten their lamps. May Thy blessings rest upon this state government, in its legislative, executive and judicial activities, that all may be for each, and each may be for all. May the golden star above the golden torch of the flag of this state shine forever, and may it contribute much to the perfect union of the stars of America. Amen.

Note: The flag of the state mentioned in this prayer is that of Indiana.

* * * *

Thanksgiving

For the serenity of Christian faith amid the turmoil of mundane chaos, we thank Thee. We thank Thee for the spiritual inheritance of this nation. We thank Thee for the historical heritage of Thy church. Above all we thank Thee for that which makes us Christian. Help us to maintain our integrity, to trust in Thy promise, and to nourish clean thoughts, to the end that we may be thankful even in disappointment, distress and despair. We thank Thee, O Lord, for Thy word that dispels the dark experiences in human life. For all of these, and for more, we thank Thee, in our savior's name. Amen.

Scripture: Psalm 26.

Tree of Life

O God, the only God, the true God, our shield, our rock and our refuge, we praise Thy name. Implant in our hearts the tree of the cross. May it be ever green and ever fruitful. Nourish the tree with Thy grace. May it be ever strong and ever prosperous. Help us to look up unto that tree in distress. Enable us to behold that tree in turmoil. Let it be our guide, our friend and our all. In our redeemer's name we pray. Amen.

Scriptures: Psalm 1:1-3; Jeremiah 17:7-8.

Note: The tree of life in the garden of Eden makes one think of the tree which is likened to the saintly man. A Christian should be like the tree of the cross, for it is the source of eternal life.

* * * * *

Truth

O God, help us to think intelligently. We thank Thee for Thy word. We thank Thee for Thy creation. May we be intelligently religious. May we be intelligently moral. May we be intelligently intellectual. Above all, grant us the courage to abide by the truth. So let us act according to Thy act. Let us live according to Thy precepts. Let us serve according to Thy law. Glory be to the crown of the Christ, in whose name we pray. Amen.

Scripture: Psalm 15.

Note: This psalm contains eleven principles of practical life, and is said to be a summary of all 613 laws of early Judaism. Note that these principles are teachings, and not laws in the accepted sense.

Truth

We thank Thee, O Lord, for our glorious consciousness of Thy presence in the temporal darkness of human turmoil. Towering above the mundane chaos of vanities and transgressions, let there arise within us Christian faith, hope and love. Help us to realize more fully that salvation is from Thee, not from man. Grant us that silent power of truth which has become manifest in Christ Jesus. In his name. Amen.

Scripture: Psalm 62.

Note: There are several words translated "truth" in the Bible. The common Hebrew word for it means reliability or dependability, whereas the Greek word for it connotes that which is real or actual. In the New Testament, however, the Greek word often signifies that which is sure or valid. "Amen" comes from the same root, from which the Hebrew word for "truth" is derived.

Wisdom

O God, let the firmament of heaven be shattered. Let the foundations of the earth burst. We cling to Thee, O rock of salvation, for we have dedicated ourselves to Thee, and we believe in Thy word. May our conduct be righteous and kind. May our speech be humble and gracious. May our thoughts be clear and clean. May we, above all, gain Christian wisdom. To the everlasting cross be glory, forever and ever. Amen.

Scriptures: Proverbs 4:7-9; 21:21-31; Ephesians 3:7-13.

Note: "Wisdom" in the Bible is not the accumulated knowledge of books, but rather the ability to translate God's will into life. The Hebrew word for "wisdom" and the Greek word for it both have the sense of skill, even though this connotation is not always applicable.

Wisdom

Our Father in heaven, hallowed be Thy name. We thank Thee for Thy word that has become flesh. Help us to grow intelligent and wise in Thy sight. Forbid that we remain ignorant and foolish about Thy wisdom. Let it rule over us. Enable us to actualize thus Christian principles of life. In our savior's name. Amen.

Scriptures: Proverb 16:22-33; John 1:14-18; James 3:13-18.

* * * * *

Our heavenly Father, we praise Thy name. Help us to gain the intelligence that pierces through the veil before the truth. Enable us to attain the virtue that breaks through the curtain before the good. May we, above all, cultivate piety that will tear through the clouds before Thy countenance. Grant that we truly become Thy sons and daughters. Through Jesus Christ, Our lord. Amen.

Scripture: Proverb 15:2-10.

Note: The contrast between the wise and the foolish is given in the above scripture. A wise man is a person who knows how to apply God's will to actual life. "Piety" in this prayer signifies religious devotion.

Wisdom

We thank Thee, our Father, for these words of Job. Thy wisdom transcends chemical formulae and physical equipment. Thy wisdom exceeds commercial appraisal and monetary price. Help us to understand that Thou alone knowest it, and without Thee it does not exist. Enable us to comprehend that this wisdom is primarily religious and essentially moral. May the fear of the Lord, acknowledged through the Christ, cause us to 'depart from sins and transgressions to the end that the cross may be glorified. In our savior's name we pray. Amen.

Scripture: Job 28:12-28.

Note: In Biblical Hebrew, there is no word for "religion." This concept is expressed by "the fear of the Lord" as in Job 28:28; and Proverb 1:7. However, in later Hebrew there are other words used for "religion."

Wisdom

We thank Thee, O God, for that wisdom which transcends time and space. Help us to gain that wisdom which comprehends the creative order of the universe. Enable us to attain that wisdom which underlies the wondrous miracle of life. May our human knowledge accord itself with that divine wisdom which became flesh in Christ Jesus. In his name. Amen.

Scripture: Proverb 8:22-36.

Note: This is one of the most significant sections of the Proverbs, in which God's wisdom is personified. It is something like the "word" in John 1:1-13, though they are not exactly alike.

* * * *

O God, the heavens declare Thy glory, and the firmament showeth Thy handiwork. We thank Thee for our urge for the good, the true and the beautiful. Enable us to actualize this urge in sharing the fortunes and misfortunes of all mankind. Give us the intelligence to distinguish between the good and the bad, between the true and the false, and between the beautiful and the ugly. May this intelligence guide us in attaining Christian grace and virtues. Let Thy glory manifest itself through us, if it be Thy will. Let us serve Thee for Christ's sake. Amen.

Note: The opening section of this prayer is taken from Psalm 19:1.